ACCELERATE

A GUIDED PLAYBOOK FOR YOUNG DREAMERS, SCHOLARS, ARTISTS, AND ATHLETES

ZIZ ABDUR RA'OOF
LIL BARCASKI

We dedicate this book to all the teachers, parents, mentors, and counselors who work tirelessly to make our lives better.

Accelerate

A Guided Playbook for Young Dreamers, Scholars, Artists, and Athletes

By Ziz Abdur Ra'oof and Lil Barcaski

ISBN: 878-1-7336929-4-6

Published by: GWN Publishing

www.ghostwritersnetwork.com

Cover Design: Cyndi Long – GFAD Design / LongBar Creative Solutions

www.longbarcreatives.com

WHAT PEOPLE ARE SAYING ABOUT "ACCELERATE"

Young people need to be inspired to reach their goals and dreams. "Accelerate" offers students a way to consider who they are, who they want to become, and where they want to go in life. More than just lip service and rhetoric, "Accelerate" shares a playbook full of authenticity, real-life concepts, and practical exercises that make a difference. This is a must read!

- Jon Gordon, best-selling author of *The Energy Bus* and Training Camp

---

As a licensed school psychologist, I have worked with adolescents for over 20 years. This period of life can be filled with a great deal of angst, because although high school students want to be independent and follow their dreams after they graduate, at the same time they often flounder on how to do that and what they want their future look to look like. Accelerate is a wonderful resource, with real life scenarios and practical exercises that help adolescents identify their personal strengths, develop a positive sense of self, and develop specific personal and post-secondary goals.

Activities lead adolescents in becoming self-aware of potential fears, bad habits, and counterproductive relationships that interfere with their ability to achieve their vision. It then helps students to identify their gifts and talents, as well as develop an open mindset mentality and highlight personal values. It gives them a path on how to find mentors and professionals that can be their support network to help them develop a brand for themselves to achieve their goals.

We use this resource as part of our Transition 2 College program because it is a very practical, step by step guide to assist student to choose vocational paths as they apply to college or other post-secondary options.

I highly recommend this resource to adolescents as well as programs that work with high school students to assist in creating their path to independence and a fulfilling life.

- Alicia N. Braccia PsyD, ABSNP, LSP SS710
Clinical Director of Center for Health, Learning & Achievement, CHLAFL.com

---

We want all our children to feel seen, heard, and valued for who they are so they can use their strengths and gifts to make the world a better place. Kids need role models to follow. They need connection with as many caring adult mentors as possible. Let Ziz Abdur-Ra'oof be "that amazing coach" for your child. His love, care, and student-centered storytelling jump off the page right into your heart and down into your feet.

Accelerate: A Guided Playbook for Young Dreamers, Artists, Scholars and Athletes" is life-changing book for kids, parents, families, teachers, and community to read and read together!

- Laura Gilchrist, Vice President ParentCamp

It's not easy to be a teen -- to take risks, bounce back from failure, and find your groove and your people at a time when you're still figuring out who you are and what you value. In "Accelerate," Ziz uses his extensive coaching and mentoring experience to reach teens where they are and help them become the best possible version of themselves, both now and throughout their lives.

- Phyllis L. Fagell, LCPC, school counselor, journalist, and author of "Middle School Matters"

As a psychologist and mom of four, one thing I know for sure is that more is caught than taught. In "Accelerate", Ziz and his writing partner Lil give teens a track to run on. They show teens the way to become better versions of themselves now and how to ask the questions to become lifelong learners. One of the challenges facing young people in a digital world is building relationships.

Chapter 6 explains the value of relationships and how seeking a Mentor can help navigate through the change and challenges that is part of life. Learning about the importance of discipline, values driven leadership, and entrepreneurship from a young age will be the difference that makes an impact for their future. I am excited to share "Accelerate" with my children and the young adults, I Mentor.

- Molly Geil - PhD, Retired School Psychologist & Entrepreneur

This book has the ability to make a huge difference in the lives of the students/people/teens that apply the principles outlined in it to their day to day activities. The tips suggested in this book will guide them to creating experiences that tap into the unlimited potential of human possibilities.

- Tony Dottino Author, Speaker, Business Coach
Founder of the **U.S.A. Memory Championship** -
www.usamemorychampionship.com

Young people are smart. Having worked with over 100k youth around the world I can attest to their uncanny ability to discern when the message isn't real. In *Accelerate*, Ziz not only is able to provide a message that is deeply needed but through his own life experiences he is able to present it in a way that so many young people can see themselves in and connect with. This makes the takeaways that much easier to integrate. I wish that so many of the youth I work with could meet Ziz as they inevitably are better for it...*Accelerate* is now the way that I do so.

- Jon Gordon, Co-Founder, The Piece Project, Senior Partner, HumanSide

---

I absolutely loved reading "Accelerate." It is truly powerful and such an experience. I am always encouraging the kids to try and participate in new things that may lead to something they are truly passionate about… something that gives them joy. Accelerate guides the reader paralleled with Ziz's own experiences to help bring him or her into their own, normalizing the thoughts and feelings of uncertainty. There is so much pressure as a young adult to select and choose a career path. In this book, Ziz and Lil take that step by step, suggesting some of the harder conversations with "water breaks." Loved this!

I cannot wait to share this experience with my own sons and daughter.

- Carolyn Havens, Entrepreneur, former collegiate athlete, eCommerce guru, and mom to 3 children.

I'm sure I am not alone in worrying about how to help my child succeed in life. How to reach their potential, fulfill their destiny. The biggest piece of that puzzle is helping them realize, early on, that they are capable of everything they put their mind, heart, and soul into. I am so grateful that this book, Accelerate, has been written. I feel that this book is the tool I've been looking for to help my child understand how to take action in shaping his own life. My greatest desire is for him to become an active participant in this game of life and shape it to his deepest desires for himself. I highly recommend Accelerate to any parent raising a teenager.

- Cassandra Lyn Daniel - Realtor, Entrepreneur, and Mom

CONTENTS

DON'T READ THIS...

My dearest Rookie (and I mean that affectionately because I too was a rookie years ago). I am so excited for you to read this book and these stories, and I hope that it inspires and encourages you in the early stages of your journey of life. While these stories are fictionalized, they are based on actual accounts from my life and the lives of my friends, clients, and colleagues.

I am grateful to be a part of your game(journey).

I want you to excel at being *YOU*, so let's go for a ride! Let's work at playing your best game!

Love

Ziz

PRE-GAME

IMAGE CONTRIBUTED BY
Thomas Terranova, AIA

'87 is the year I graduated from college. It represents a milestone in the lives of those who came before me and after me. In my family, I was the first college graduate. I was the first high school athlete to receive a full scholarship. I was the first Division 1 collegiate athlete and I was the first to be drafted by an NFL team (Kansas City Chiefs). For some of you, that may not seem like a big deal, however, for me and my family, it was huge.

You see — my grandmother could not even read, not because she didn't want to… it was not permitted because it was not allowed for someone of color, especially a woman to *read*. So, **'87** represents the work of those who came before me and what's possible when you get the support of your community, your forum, your posse, your tribe which is composed of teachers, mentors, coaches, family, and the surrounding community. It's a **TEAM** approach and its GAME TIME.

It's important for you to find *your tribe, your group*, your people who will support you as you go on your life's journey. People will help you……

……*Accelerate!*

We have created a playbook that is designed for group discussions and personal introspection. As you read, and after you finish, please share your favorite chapters, quotes, and excerpts on social media and tag me.

IG: @ziz87_

Twitter: @ziz87

LinkedIn: http://linkedin.com/in/zizabdurraoof

NOTE: Throughout the book, you will see a little image of a water bottle. That's for you to take a "water break," meaning a time to reflect on what we just talked about.

INTRODUCTION

You are at an interesting point in life. You're likely floating between exploring your independence and feeling frozen in place, and you're not sure what to do or how to do it. A part of you is ready to take on the world. The other part, however, might be stuck, or paralyzed by a combination of uncertainty and fear. Some days you might be full of ideas and hopes about your future, while others you might just want to sit around and play video games, make Tik Tok videos or watch YouTube all day.

You know what? That's normal.

When you were in elementary school you were most likely energetic, enthusiastic, and playful, just having fun most of the time. As you got older, you started to view your world a bit differently. You probably noticed the world is weird, wacky, full of uncertainty, and even scary at times, and you might have begun to see more fear on your horizon.

Moving forward, your middle school years and onto becoming a high school student, planning to go to college or starting your career brings about lots of transitional changes, physical, emotional, mental, geographical, and spiritual.

When I was a kid, I was fortunate to attend an awesome elementary school in Annapolis, Maryland. It was a stone's throw from the United States Naval Academy stadium. Some things from my elementary school years stand out for me. One was my first name (Toren), it was unique, different, pronounced, "torn," as in a torn piece of paper. I hated my name because of how it sounded. So, imagine my excitement when my parents told me they were changing our names. My new name became Zizuddin or Ziz for short. I gotta admit, sometimes, I embraced my nickname and sometimes I didn't

You might be wondering, why the name change? My parents were going through a spiritual makeover and I didn't know or understand why at the time. I was just happy to be getting a new name. When you are 11 or 12 years old, you don't really understand the significance of a religious shift. Without knowing at the time, my new name and religion played a pivotal role in developing my identity. I totally bought into what my name meant - Grows in faith. One of the most important lessons I learned from new religion came from fasting. My first time fasting took place during the summer of my 9th grade year of high school. It delayed me from starting football practice on time with the rest of the team and I think some guys resented me for that. Just imagine, being a bit of an outcast on a team before you even start practice.

As I look back, fasting taught me several things. First of all, I looked at fasting as a gift rather than a burden. It was a wonderful opportunity for me to build up my spiritual muscle. I'm not sure about you, but I needed to build in that area. Fasting taught me:

Commitment
Consistency
Discipline
Focus

These are qualities that helped me in school with my academics, athletics, and arts. Unknowingly, it also taught me how to take a stand, be alone, and be comfortable with myself. That gift didn't occur to me right away, it appeared many years later in life as I continued to work on my spiritual muscle and consistency.

The other big shift was moving from Annapolis to Pasadena, Maryland, a very different kind of community. Middle school started in sixth grade at my new school, so I went from being a sixth grader (an upperclassman) in an elementary school to the bottom of the rung in a middle school of sixth, seventh, and eighth graders who I didn't know and who didn't know me.

My world got flipped around in more ways than one. My new school had serious cultural issues (or as they were called back then, RACE issues). I was completely confused. If you were to see my class pictures from my elementary school, you'd see that it looked and acted more like the United Nations of Harmony. Let's just say, when a white kid at my new school said, "you better protect yourself because there could be a RACE riot," I was a bit naïve and surprised. It was my first experience with racism.

As I look back, I was definitely shielded and protected by my tribe, some looked like me and some that did not. My different name and the fact that I was tall and athletic for a middle schooler helped ease my way through this interesting transition.

Some of my white friends wondered why the things their parents had told them about people who looked like me didn't ring true. I was a bit of a paradox to them and they were perplexed. It raised questions for them about what their parents were saying and who to believe.

Thank goodness for my (tribe), teachers, coaches, and family who were awesome because they created an environment where I felt welcomed and comfortable in and out of class so I could learn despite some of the "isms" that popped up in and out of the school and town. My academic and athletic abilities were developing, yet it was the care and concern I expressed for others that made me *different* and caused others to look at me in a way they didn't look at other students.

I was a sensitive young man who was comfortable enough in his own skin to stand out and do the right things. I was involved in various activities in the school thanks to the many teachers who encouraged and protected me from the harsh reality of the times.

To this day, I can name most of my teachers because they made a positive impact on my life at a crucial time of my development. I was encouraged to dream, to pursue and set my life goals, and to be involved in high school. So, I lived in both worlds, academics and athletics, and even dabbled as a Thespian. That was a choice that went against my norm, which was to run track my junior year. This was a sport I was good at. Instead, I chose to do something different. I wanted a new experience that was outside my wheelhouse. So, I played Officer Krupke in the musical West Side Story. It was the experience of a lifetime that taught me presence, timing, and reinforced the team concept from another perspective. Being a member of the Thespian Troupe was a fun and incredibly rewarding experience, and one of the hardest things I did during my high school years . The icing on the proverbial cake for me was the support I received from other athletes, student body members, and coaches on opening night. There were times in school when I did not perform my best academically. It was tough juggling the demands of school, family, friends, and being pulled in many different directions. At times, I lacked the confidence and mindset to excel to my best in athletics.

(Water Break = Reflection Time) Have you tried an activity, club, subject where you were not as talented or gifted?

Talent is just one piece of the puzzle -- the drive to succeed is another.

Having reached the NFL was a huge achievement for me that only 1% of football players reach. My success was not mine alone, it was a TEAM approach, my tribe, my coaches, my teachers, my mentors, and my family.

It was my '87!

Whether you are participating in Band, Robotics, Computer Club, SGA, Dance Troupe, Musicals, a Thespian or playing Sports it's all part of who you are and will shape who you become. My involvement in various activities in middle and high school taught me many lessons and skills that I carry with me today. I call them transferrable LIFE skills and lessons:

Have a Game Plan,
Take Action,
Fail, Learn & Adjust
And...
ACCELERATE!

Introduction

Just like a team needs a game plan to win, this book can be your game plan that launches you through your middle and HS school years, and beyond.

A NOTE FROM AUTHOR LIL BARCASKI

I always wanted to be writer. I started writing at an early age and knew this was my path. That is… until someone very close to me told me I had no talent and to consider something else for a career. I was heartbroken, struck down, and humiliated.

So, I stopped writing. I did lots of other things that were fun and interesting, but not as awesome as writing. I let those comments change my life's course. Many years later, I was tasked to do some writing for work, and I was told a different story.

"Wow, Lil, you're a terrific writer." I started hearing that a lot. I started to believe in my dream of being a writer again.

Now, many more years later, I get to write books like this one with awesome people like Ziz. And I write all kinds of books, from fiction to self-help. My name is on many published books with 5-star reviews and happy comments from people that love what I write, and I get to move people with my words.

I'm often tasked to help people write their memoirs and tell THEIR stories. Those books are my favorites.

Ziz and I wrote this book because we want you to find YOUR story. It's going to be a great one.

So, I hope you enjoy this book. Do all the exercises. Consider the concepts and ideas we've put forth carefully and take away the things that will help you on your path. We want you to figure out who you are and what matters to you. We want you to be successful in whatever way you define that to be. We're with you all the way.

...... Accelerate!

A CAUTIONARY TALE: THE TWO MARITZAS

Maritza 1:

Maritza 1 is 24 years old. She was a C student in high school and did not participate in many extracurricular activities. Her favorite subject was home economics and she always made an A in those classes. She was a cheerleader in her freshman and sophomore years but dropped out in junior year because she wanted to get a job. Most of her friends were other cheerleaders but she lost touch with them after she quit the team. She still works at Starbucks as a barista, the same job she's had since high school. She's been offered management positions, but she doesn't have the confidence to move up. She's comfortable making coffee and running the register but doesn't socialize with the people that work there who are mostly younger than she is. Most of the work friends she had moved on after high school when they went on to college.

She has a boyfriend but he's not very nice to her. He broke up with her, then changed his mind and she allowed him to come back. She hasn't many friends because most of them don't like him.

She has an older car and it often breaks down, but it gets her from place to place.

She was sharing an apartment with a friend but the last time her car broke down, she had to pay a lot to get it fixed. She asked her parents if she could move back home and they reluctantly said, yes.

When she is not at work, she spends time watching You Tube videos and playing on Facebook.

One thing she does like to do is bake, but now that she lives at her parents, she feels like she is intruding by using their kitchen and her mom is always on a diet and doesn't like having cookies and cakes around the house.

Maritza 1 is not very happy with her life. She sleeps too much, doesn't exercise, and sneaks out to eat fast food more often than she should. She daydreams of having a home of her own and a good job, but she doesn't have much Identity Capital and has no idea how to move forward to improve her situation.

Maritza 2:

Maritza 2 is 24 years old. She was a B + student in high school and participated in variety of different extracurricular activities including, drama club where she performed in a few of the school plays. She was on the girls' varsity basketball team and was on the Yearbook committee in her senior year. Maritza 2 had a lot of different kinds of friends in high school and got along with a very diverse group of people. She didn't go to college and still works at Starbucks, a job she's had since high school, but she's the day manager at the store now. She takes classes in business administration at the community college at night and, in her spare time, works on her side hustle business making one of a kind jewelry that she sells at craft shows and online. She hopes to make that her full-time business someday.

She had a boyfriend, but he wasn't very nice to her, so she broke up with him, and though he begged for a second chance, she would not allow him to come back. She has many friends from work and stays in touch with her high school friends as well. She studies with some of her college friends and goes out for coffee and drinks with them often, sharing ideas about school and work.

She has a small affordable car and shares a nice, three-bedroom, house with one of her best friends. They use the extra bedroom in the house for her jewelry making and an office space for them both to study and where her friend can work on the novel she is writing in her spare time. They get along very well and are both ambitious and motivated to help one another become successful.

Maritza 1 is very happy with her life. She sleeps and eats well and gets plenty of exercise. She has been building her Identity Capital since high school and continues to do so as she moves toward her future.

Which of these two Maritza's would you like to be in the future?

LIFE IS A LADDER

"Your time is limited, so don't waste it living someone else's life."

- Steve Jobs

CONSIDER THAT OUR LADDER REPRESENTS LIFE AND EACH RUNG ON the ladder indicates where you are on your life's journey. The irony is that sometimes you slip or continue to repeat various steps of your journey up the ladder. One of the many questions you need to continuously ask yourself is *where am I on this ladder?*

- What rung am I on?
- Where am I going?
- Do I have enough resources to help me get there?
- Am I climbing at the right pace?

The Tale of Two Thomases
Thomas 1 wants to be a doctor.

He has a school friend named Joe whose mom is a doctor. He's not sure what kind of doctor she is but, man, she has a great car. Joe's mom took Joe, Thomas, and two other friends to the Bahama's on spring break vacation and paid for everything.

She's rich, Thomas thought as he boarded the cruise ship. *Being a doctor must be a great way to become rich. I should be a doctor.*

Thomas 1 watches lots of TV shows about doctors; *Greys Anatomy, The Good Doctor,* even *Doctor Who*. He plays the video game, Horror Hospital 2 (but mostly he plays Fortnite). He takes the basic required high school courses in math and science and is a solid C plus student. He is a junior in high school and is planning to apply for colleges over the summer and has some idea of the schools he thinks he might want to attend.

He plays trumpet in the high school band but doesn't belong to any other groups or clubs and is not involved in any community activities.

Thomas 1 has picked out the kind of car he will drive when he becomes a doctor, a sweet Corvette convertible. He tells several girls at school that he is planning to be a doctor. A couple of them are willing to go on a date with him, based on the concept that he has it together and that he has a plan for his future. He thinks he's set and that his future is so bright he needs to wear shades.

What rung do you think he is he on?

Thomas 2 wants to be a doctor.

Thomas 2 was twelve-years-old when his beloved grandmother died of heart disease. Thomas 2 was very upset when he overheard a conversation between his mom and dad and found out that his grand-mother might have been helped by better doctors and medicines that she couldn't afford. She might have lived longer if new treatments had been available to her or she had more money. He vowed to become a doctor, a heart specialist, and to do research to improve treatments for heart disease.

Thomas 2 watches very little TV. He is in honors science and math classes and studies a lot. He volunteers at the local hospital and has asked a doctor there to be his mentor. Dr. Adams was thrilled when asked and meets with Thomas twice a month to give him advice, recommend books and videos he should watch, and has written a college recommendation for Thomas.

Thomas 2 is a junior in high school and narrowed his choice of colleges down to five he knows are great bets for a pre-med program. He is applying to all of them and will even apply to two other lesser choices as a back-up plan.

He is a solid A minus student (mostly because he isn't great at English and History but he's working on improving those grades). He's an officer in the SGA, played George in the drama clubs' production of "Our Town," and helps out at the local food bank on Saturday mornings and every holiday where he and his family serve the homeless.

What rung do you think he is he on?

Have you ever thought about the connection between knowing who you are and achieving success? This concept implies that you know yourself. Do you have any idea what success means to you, and how will you achieve it? What does success look like? What do you think you will have if you are successful?

- A great job?
- A lot of money?
- A happy relationship or family of your own?
- A beautiful home or fancy car?
- Doing something powerful and positive that makes a difference in the world?

You don't need to know all the answers yet. You have time on your side and that's a great thing to have. One of the many great things about being you, right this very minute, is that you are at a place in your life where you get to explore all the possibilities and get to discover YOU; who you are, what you want, who you want to be and how you want to live your one unique life.

You can take time to reflect. You can uncover the things that actually make you happy; what you like and dislike, what you can be proud of, what you want to share with the world.

You get to create YOUR OWN STORY.

Your story, not your parents, grandparents, or family's story - Your Story.

Who Are You Really?

When asked the question, "Who are you?" People may answer:

- I am a student
- I'm a gamer
- I'm a member of the band/choir
- I'm an athlete
- I'm an artist or musician

Those are things you enjoy, and they are also things you participate in. Some of those things can define you and might be the definition you carry through life. If you see yourself as a musician, an artist, an athlete, and that is your life's path, those things might help shape and define you. Being an athlete shaped me. My writing partner defined herself as a musician and a writer. We, like our book's graphic artist, also define ourselves as entrepreneurs. We know we like to carve out our own pathways and prefer to work for ourselves rather than be part of the corporate world. Each of us have pretty much always felt that way. We have a high level of fierce independence. Later in this book, we will talk about the "gig economy" and how many young people are taking entrepreneurism to a new level, creating their own "jobs" rather than waiting to be hired. Does that sound like you?

If you have aspirations to be a scientist, doctor, nurse, financier, or are considering a career path like accountant, plumber, electrician, those are jobs that will be a big part of who you are and will shape you. But careers are not all of what makes you who you are. Your ideals, passions, loves, likes and dislikes, talents and abilities, and especially your values are the greater part of you.

The quote by Jobs at the start of this chapter challenges you to stop pretending to be someone you're not. Take full advantage of this tip by using your time to reflect, develop, and create who you want to be. If you are like a lot of people your age, you spend a lot of time online, engaging in gaming and social media. You might confuse the virtual world with the real world at times. That's okay. Lots of people do but start to think about it. Are your "friends" on Instagram, Snap Chat, Facebook, and online gaming groups actual friends or are they virtual ones?

Confusing isn't it?

Recently, one of my yoga students shared with me that he considered me lucky to be in a different generation. I asked him why he thought this, and he said, "Because you all use social media as a tool to eventually connect with people in-person, but my generation uses it as our primary way to communicate." He went on to say that it's confusing and complex at times. "I would rather just have someone tell me what they're thinking instead of using emoticons, pictures, and abbreviated words that really don't tell me much."

So, what do you think the story of the two Thomases is trying to tell us?

Do you think that Thomas 1 has a chance of becoming a doctor? Is he living in reality? Is he engaging in real life events that will lead him to that career?

What about his values? Is he becoming a doctor for the right reasons?

Thomas 2 sees being a doctor as far more than a career. He sees it as something that defines a big part of who he wants to be.

Can you understand the difference?

Chapter One Exercises:

What goal do you think you want to achieve?

What rung are you on based on what you have done to move toward your goal?

What can you do to move up a few rungs? Draw yourself on the ladder now. Draw what rung you think you can get to this year, next year, in two years.

Write down three possible career paths you think you might enjoy taking:

1. _____
2. _____
3. _____

Now explore each of those paths.

What are the advantages of each career? (Ex. Good pay, lots of room to grow)

What are the disadvantages? (Ex. Years of study, not many job opportunities)

Pick any of these career possiblities. Name three things you could do to help you climb the rungs of the ladder towards achieving your career goal they way that Thomas two did.

1. _____

2. _____

3. _____

Accelerate

FINDING YOUR GROOVE

THE STORY OF TWO SUNNYS

Sunny 1:

Sunny 1 just graduated eighth grade and is spending the summer relaxing. She sleeps each morning until 10 am then rolls out of bed and eats some cereal with chocolate milk, her favorite. Her mom asks her to do a few chores around the house, but she doesn't usually get them finished, and when mom comes in from work, she is disappointed and angry.

When asked what classes she might want to take in high school she says art and music. She plays piano. She's been taking piano lessons since fifth grade, but she doesn't practice much. She doesn't really have to. It just comes naturally to her, but she isn't really that interested in getting better. *I'm good enough,* she thinks. *No reason to stress myself out and get better at it.*

She really loves to draw. She doodles and draws on everything, but she isn't very good at it. She thinks taking a few classes in high school will help her get better, but she mostly likes to sit on the couch, binge watch old sitcoms on Netflix, and draw mindlessly. She's comfortable where she's at with her skills.

Sunny 2:

Sunny 2 just graduated eighth grade and is spending the summer doing a few interesting things. She gets up every morning at about 8 am. She goes downstairs and eats a good breakfast, sometimes cereal with skim milk, sometimes oatmeal or yogurt. After breakfast, she goes to the chalkboard next to the fridge and looks at the tasks her mom has for her for that day. She accomplishes all of her chores before lunch. Then she practices her piano lesson for 45 minutes. She's been taking piano lessons since fifth grade and she is very good. It comes to her naturally, but she knows if she puts a little time in, she can be really good at it. Her uncle is a professional piano player and makes a good living at it. She thinks that's a cool way to make money if she ever needs to.

Sunny 2 really enjoys art. She knows she isn't as naturally talented at art as she is at piano, but it makes her happy. Every afternoon, she sets up her paints and drawing tools and watches *How To* videos on art techniques. She is going to a two-week summer art camp and she's already chosen the art classes she plans to take in high school. She believes if she works at it, she can get really good at some form of art and make it her career. It's a struggle, but she thinks it's worth it.

The big challenge for you, right now, is figuring what really works for you. The opportunities in front of you will have a great impact on your life. You are essentially standing in front of many doors, and as you make choices, either a door may open for you or close right in front of you.

Imagine you are creating a picture from scratch. You have a blank canvas and you're the artist. Let that really sink in... YOU are the author of your STORY, the painter of your own life's picture.

"My life didn't please me, so, I created my life."

Coco Chanel

Over the years you have been influenced by many people. Parents, siblings, aunts, uncles, grandparents, cousins, neighbors, and many others have impacted your life. The first seven years of your life you were a human recording machine. Some of that programming will serve you well as you move forward, and some will not.

As you contemplate, where you are in life and, like we said in Chapter 1, what rung of the ladder you are on, you will face commentary from your family, friends, allies, and individuals who do not always have your best interest in mind.

Ultimately, your high school years are a great place to practice and to develop your thinking. Reflect on things that cause you frustration, angst, and even anger. Take note of those things and conversely, vigorously write notes on the things that bring you happiness, fulfillment, and great joy.

"If you can't learn to master your thinking, you're in deep trouble forever."

- Elizabeth Gilbert

"Our doubts are traitors and make us lose the good we oft might win, by fearing to attempt."

— **William Shakespeare**

It's a Matter of Perspective

High school offers you a great opportunity to figure yourself out.

- What are you interested in?
- What are you good at?
- What do people consider your best talents?
- What do you love to do or hate to do?

When you take the time to look at yourself from different angles, you start to see a variety of pictures of who you are and who you might become.

Try this. Find a picture that's hanging on any wall. Stand ten feet away from the picture. Now stand five feet away. Now two then one foot away. Get as close to the picture as you can.

Take time to really see it. Now move to one side and then the other. Look at the picture from every distance and angle you can.

Interesting right? The picture is different from every position. You see different elements. Yet, it's the same picture, right?

That's you.

If you can think about yourself in different ways, see yourself from different angles, you're going to see different parts of yourself. Your possibilities are endless. You just need to dig a little deeper and spend some time learning about you.

Processing is Uncomfortable

You're going to discover some great things about yourself and probably some things you don't like or may not be proud of. You might find that you resist some things, have prejudices that aren't attractive. You may realize that even if you love doing something, you may not have what it takes to earn a living at that particular thing.

Let's say you love to sing but you don't have a natural talent for singing. You may be able to hone that skill enough to make a career of it. You may not. Singing might be a hobby but not a life plan.

Lots of people want to go into gaming, mostly because they like to play video games. The same thing applies to sports. Not everyone will make it in a career in either of those things but that doesn't mean there is no way to enjoy those things or even find ways to make gaming or sports part of your career.

If you love music but don't have the necessary skills to be the next superstar, did you know that there are dozens of careers in music that don't require you to be a great musician?

Sound engineering, entertainment lawyer, music talent agent, producer, are all possible jobs in the industry. There is always a way to connect what you love to what you're good at. But first, you have to discover what you're good at and make that connection.

High school is a great time to discover what your interests are, to discover new talents, and to build on your existing talents.

Can you see your future in your mind? What does it look like?

Do you have self-doubts?

Yes?

Good. That's normal.

No?

Good for you. That's rare and you're a lucky duck.

Pretty much all of us experience self-doubt but we can't allow that to hold us back. If we did, we wouldn't have the innovations we have today. We wouldn't grow or excel at anything.

Like I said, processing is uncomfortable and so is growing and learning. You've heard the expression, growing pains, right? If you're in high school, you're likely to experience those growing pains, not just in your bones and muscles but in your heart and soul.

This processing, this learning and growing can cause anxiety and stress. You may not be able to express that you are feeling stress. It may be hard to define and explain to your parents, teachers, siblings, and friends. You may experience some sort of panic attacks.

Sometimes, your chest may feel tight or you may feel like it's hard to breath. That's not weird. It's something most people go through but if you are having those feelings, do your best to express that to someone, particularly your parents.

When you're feeling stress, remember to take deep breaths and most importantly remember that they are just *feelings.* Most of the time, nothing really bad is happening, it just FEELS like it is.

Working mindfully and courageously through our self-doubts is the way we go through that wave. Once you get through it, you discover the beginnings of self-belief.

How many times in your lifetime has someone asked you the very simple question, "Who are you?"

You've likely answered that question a number of different ways.

- You've answered with your name (I'm Joe Smith).
- You've declared that you are your mother or father's son or daughter (I'm John's daughter).
- You've said you are a student at such and such school (I go to school here).

- You've said you are your sibling's sibling (I'm Tisha's sister/brother).
- You've identified your position (Oh! I just got hired here).

You're a brother or sister, daughter, or son. You might define yourself by what you love, dancer, singer, student, athlete, gamer.

What if you start to think of yourself in terms of adjectives like, gifted, curious, kind, caring, smart, funny, wise?

If you start to spend time thinking about who you really are, you might begin to see yourself through the reflection of others; how they might see you. Self-awareness is a tricky thing. It's not easy to see oneself. Sometimes, you get what we call a revelation and you suddenly "see" something about yourself you may love or hate.

One way to mark those times is to start a journal. Make notes. Write down those little revelations so you can come back to them later and see how valid they are as you grow. You might be inclined to write down some goals when you have a new insight. We hope that the exercises and concepts in this book will serve as a workbook to help you discover your God-given talents and how to translate those talents into goals but first we need to discover how to stave off and fight self-doubt.

"Self-doubt kills talent." - Edie McClurg

Exercises for Chapter 2:

Answer the Following Questions:

- What do you <u>suck</u> at that you hate?
- What do you suck at but like/enjoy doing and wish you were better at or would like to learn more about?
- What are good at but aren't that interested in or don't like or care about much?

- What are you good at and love doing?

Now, create a diagram of those things and where they intersect – Somewhere in there is your possible future.

Name 5 things and/or people that are the biggest influencers in your life. This can be a person like a teacher or relative, it could be a type of music you listen to, or the kinds of movies you watch.

1. _____
2. _____
3. _____
4. _____
5. _____

What are the first 5 things that come to you when you hear the word stress?

1. _____
2. _____
3. _____
4. _____
5. _____

What is the one thing you want most from your parents?

_____

_____

_____

3

THE "WHAT IF'S?"

SELF-DOUBT IS ONE OF THE MAJOR OBSTACLES TO LIVING THE LIFE you truly deserve. This unhealthy food for the soul drags down your spirit, crushes your ambitions, and prevents you from achieving all that you can.

We all have that inner voice in our head that tells us we are not good enough, not strong enough, and that we're incapable of doing the things we dream about. Often, these feelings of weakness or incompetence come from something we learned when we were little and those false ideas become part of us. Everyone handles this differently.

I want to tell you a story about a young genius who, despite having every reason to be crippled by self-doubt, learned to share his talents with the world:

A four-year-old boy was sitting at home, playing with his toys. He was hungry, but he didn't tell anyone. He was tired, but only his posture would have shown that he was. At four years old, he couldn't or wouldn't speak. Every day, his family wondered, "What's wrong with this boy? Is he mentally disabled?"

When he started school, his teachers and classmates thought he was a dunce. They tried to teach him art and languages, but he didn't pick these things up like the other kids did. He only learned enough German to get by.

In high school, he constantly repeated his sentences to himself. Everyone thought he was slow. He applied to college, but failed the entrance exams. Eventually, he earned his degree, but couldn't get the teaching job he wanted, so he spent his days working in a boring patent office.

But, through the many years growing up, even though he was thought of as a nobody, capable of nothing, the young man told himself a different story. He knew he was good at something, and that something was science.

That young man was Albert Einstein and, in 1905, he shared four ideas that would become the foundation of modern physics.

Einstein was a genius. We all know that today, but it couldn't have been further from obvious in his formative years.

Did he make the impact on the world he did just because he was smart? Does intelligence shine through despite the odds? Probably not. Many brilliant people never overcome the hurdles of feeling they like they don't belong.

Brilliance was one critical ingredient in the Einstein formula, but an equally important element was his ability to overcome his self-doubt and keep working.

Today, there's convincing evidence that how well you perform in life depends a lot on how much you believe you can improve when it seems like you're not achieving anything.

Tips for Dealing with Self-Doubt

Live in the Present

Most of the time, feelings of self-doubt are attached to memories of times in the past when you failed to achieve something or when a school mate or teacher told you that you were not good enough. Don't dwell on those moments. Think about the person you are now. Learning to live in the present and not the past will destroy self-doubt every time. Think about all the things you couldn't do when you were small that you can do now that you've grown. You don't just grow in size. You grow in ability, intellect, and talent.

Couldn't do something once?

That was then. Try it again. Try it until you can. Athletes, musicians, scientists… they all know what this means.

Trust in Yourself

Sometimes we can be our own worst enemies. If you tell yourself that you can't do something, then you probably won't allow yourself to succeed at it. Have faith in yourself, tell yourself that you are just as capable as the next person of achieving your dreams, and stop listening to the voice inside that keeps saying "I can't."

A famous minister and author Norman Vincent Peale wrote a book many years ago called, *The Power of Positive Thinking*. That book affected many people and helped them live fuller, happier lives. The basic concept of that book is summed up in one of his most famous quotes.

"What the mind can conceive and believe, and the heart desire, you can achieve."

Think it! Believe it! Achieve it!

Got it?

Fight the Negative with the Positive

At times it seems like the negative voices in your head are louder than the positive voices. They say that you're not good enough or that someone else is better. But the positive voices can drown those thoughts out if you let them.

Try to catch this when it happens and tell yourself a different story:

I *can* do it.

I *am* good enough.

I *am* awesome.

Work to counteract the negative thoughts with positive energy. When you feel a negative thought coming on, simply remind yourself about the things you like about yourself, your strengths, and all the things you have achieved in your life and are proud of.

- Studying comes easily to me and I love studying.
- I have a good memory .
- There are many subjects I like and I'm good at.
- I like to exercise regularly and eat properly.
- I understand that habits make a person and I know how to develop good habits.
- I know that friends and friendships make a huge impact on my life and I am careful about how I choose my friends.
- I'm a good student and I'm getting better each and every day.
- I know how to prepare for tests. I am a good test taker and I love taking tests.
- I take my education seriously and I study hard so I can have a successful future.
- I have some great, God-given talents and I am working to hone the skills and talents I have.

Become your own best friend and champion

Loving yourself is important. If you don't become your own best friend and love yourself, who else will?

If you don't have confidence in what you do, and don't trust yourself and your own instincts, why should anyone else?

There's a superhero in all of us. Find your superpowers, believe in them, and trust yourself. There are no limits to what you can do, who you can become, if you have faith in the most important person in your life... YOU!

The Elimination Game

Once you beat the self-doubt monster, you can begin to get a handle on what you're truly good at and you can start to eliminate things that aren't a great fit for your future career, business or life. Some things will become hobbies and some things will become part-time side hustles, work that you do on the side for extra income, but that may not become your life's work.

Some things will turn out to be duds. Some dreams are not meant to be, and others will surface when you least expect them to.

Some people never realize they have an amazing talent. I have a friend who joined the school choir in his freshman year of high school just to please a girl he liked. The choir lacked male voices, so he showed up to auditions just to be near her. He had no idea he could sing. No one had ever asked him to. Turned out he had perfect pitch and the voice of an angel. He wound up singing professionally for many years. Talents will surface and surprise the hell out of you.

I have another friend who loved to sing. She stood in line to audition for American Idol for hours, convinced that she would get a chance to sing on the show.

At the preliminary auditions, she finally got the chance to show off her voice, not for the famous people but for the people who vet the singers; the first rung of the journey. She planned to sing the national anthem.

She began… "Oh say can you see."

That's as far as she got.

"Thank, you. Next!" was the response.

In six notes, the talent scouts knew her voice wasn't good enough and sent her packing. She may not have been born to be a famous singer after all. While that was a little soul crushing, it was also enlightening. She's a nurse now and a happy and great one at that. She still sings at Karaoke often and in the church choir.

Sometimes self-awareness can help you change plans. Sometimes it can motivate you to get moving, to improve, to study like hell and get better at the thing you really believe is your calling in life.

Getting Good at Things

Once you push self-doubt out of the picture, you make room for yourself to get good at things.

If you have some serious ability or talent, no matter how good you are at that skill, there is always room to improve.

If your love for something is so strong, that may be the thing that motivates you to greatness. Like Einstein, you will have to push through, keep working at it. They say that if you put 10,000 hours into anything, work at something you desire to be good at for 10,000 hours, you will, by default, become an expert at it.

I have to say that I think there are certain things that may require a little help from that God-given talent thing but regardless, whether you have some talent or no talent for something, there is always room to improve.

Some of the greatest actors alive still take acting lessons. In every profession from realtor to massage therapist to doctor or lawyer, there are continuing education courses. People who create code for software are constantly learning new languages. Dancers are constantly learning new steps and working to leap higher, move more effectively. No matter what you choose to be "good at," never think you are done growing. There is always one more level, one more step, one more improvement or adjustment, one more skill to learn.

Dream job, dream life. What does it look like?

Once you've eliminated some things, listed some possibilities, and considered what might be a potential path, can you describe what your life might be like?

What kind of job will you have? What kind of family life? Where will you live? What will make you happy, proud, and successful.

You have lots of time to think about all those things. But in the meantime, try to be present. Don't let your future rob you of your present. High school will be over in a flash. It's hard to imagine that now, but it will be a thing in your past before you know it. While you're in high school and even college, you will be discovering lots of things about yourself. You'll be looking for clues to your future life. You will be making plans, lots of plans. What college will you go to? What will you major in? Will you go beyond college to graduate school in order to secure the career you want? Will you skip college to pursue other options?

Realize that the prize is in the process.

"For me, winning isn't something that happens suddenly on the field when the whistle blows and the crowds roar. Winning is something that builds physically and mentally every day that you train and every night that you dream."

Emmitt Smith - Dallas Cowboys Football Star

Sometimes the simplest notions are the most powerful. You want to do well, to achieve and to be recognized for your efforts. Today, everything moves so quickly, and technology constantly bombards us with the opinions of others. It can be easy to forget that sometimes the best way to learn is by trial and error. No one gets it completely right the first time. We're always either moving closer to our goals or further away from them. This doesn't mean that every misstep, every bump in the road should turn you around. If you keep moving forward, you make progress. It's when you confuse progress with perfection that you set yourself up for disappointments.

Perfection sounds great to work toward or try to achieve, but in reality, there is no such thing. Always strive to improve, to better yourself, be smarter, more efficient, stronger, healthier etc. But perfection is an ***unattainable*** goal and it can put a quick halt to your ability to make progress.

Focus on progress, not perfection.

What's your why, something or someone that is the reason you do anything?

What motivates you and gets you up and moving?

What is your passion, the thing that excites you?

Your happiness?

Your fun?

Your dream (Go big on this. Shoot for the moon)?

Your goals, small and big, short term, and long range?

Your definition of success?

Most of you have some sort of goal or goals you're trying to reach, even if you haven't fully formulated a long range, life goal in your mind. You might have a goal to raise your batting average, make the dance team, lose 10 pounds or exercise more, finish writing a short story or learn to play an instrument well enough to perform in front of people. Those can be short term goals; things you can achieve some success at sooner than later and continue to improve.

You may need or want to try something new, break an old habit, in order to see some success at these kinds of goals.

Long range goals are something that you hope to attain over a much longer stretch of time. These goals can be a bit vague in their scope without a defined path toward achieving the goal, a sort of general sense of wanting success at school or at a sport, be a better friend, student or maybe a better person. Even career goals like becoming a lawyer, doctor, or starting your own business are broader goals.

You can see the bigger picture of the things you want to accomplish; the things you have defined for yourself as "success." But sometimes the big picture is so big you don't know what steps to take to get you there. The goal can seem overwhelming; you may feel you don't have the time or the resources or you don't see what steps you can take to get yourself there.

You don't know where to start so you make excuses. Or the goal isn't really yours; it's something you feel like you should do. It's not *your* "why."

Don't live someone else's dream for them. That's not your responsibility.

So, maybe you don't even get started on your dream because you think you'll fail. Often, this is because you set unrealistic expectations and believe that if you're not perfect in your pursuit, you'll be a failure.

But guys, we're human. We're imperfect. It's what makes us each unique.

And awesome!

Perfection should never be the goal because the outcome will always be failure. This doesn't mean we don't set the bar high; absolutely we set the bar high.

Focus on the journey, not the destination.

Once you know your why, you need to write it down.

You need to write down the goal, the big picture you're trying to get to. You need to write down your why, the reason or reasons for wanting to achieve your goal. And you need to keep it somewhere where you can reach it, look at it to help keep you on track.

Then you need to focus on the how.

What can you do right now to help you reach your goal?

It's good to know the big goal is there, but for now, just focus on the process. To ultimately be successful, just focus on the steps along the path that will help you to reach the bigger goal.

Enjoy every step on the path that leads you to the future. Remember the ladder? Enjoy the climb.

Chapter 3 Exercises

Name something you really want to do but don't think you can accomplish.

Why? What are the obstacles that, in your mind, keep you from this goal?

What can you do to change your perception?

Name 3 things about yourself that you truly dislike?

1. _____
2. _____
3. _____

Now turn those around to something positive.

1. _____
2. _____
3. _____

Examples:

Negative: I talk too much.

Positive: I'm a good communicator with a lot to say.

Negative: I don't get as good grades as my sister does.

Positive: I am self-aware and know that while I have a lot to learn, I have the desire to do so.

4

CREATING YOUR BRAND

BEFORE WE CAN CONSIDER YOUR "BRAND," AND HOW TO GET PEOPLE to see you for who you are, we need to talk about how you see yourself. Once you get a clearer picture of "you," you can begin to decide how to present that vision to others.

When we talk about your brand, we are referring to the way you present yourself physically, intellectually, and socially.

What makes a person buy a certain product or use a certain service?

Why do you buy Coke instead of generic cola? Many people will say they like the taste of one soda over another but part of that is branding. Coke spends millions of dollars on advertising. Their logo, colors, print ads, TV commercials, and commercials you see at the movies that make you want to rush to the lobby for a soda are all carefully thought out and planned.

It may seem weird, but the fact is, people can brand themselves too. You can start thinking about that, even as a young person. The sooner you know who you are and how you want to be seen and perceived the more likely you will experience success.

In a sense, we are always "selling" ourselves. The way people see us affects things like who we become friends with, who we work with, how we get into the school we want to go to or get the job we want.

We're going to talk about social media in this chapter because it's a big part of our world today. People spend a lot of time on Instagram, SnapChat, Pinterest, LinkedIn, Tik Tok and all kinds of other platforms. We'll talk about each of them in a bit, but first let's look at the things that will help you define your personal brand.

Falling Into the Trap of Competition and Comparison

"I am in competition with no one. I run my own race. I have no desire to play the game of being better than anyone, in any way, shape or form. I just aim to improve, to be better than I was before. That's me and I am free." — Jenny G. Perry

---

There is no one else like you. You need to embrace this fact. That's a wonderful and powerful thing. You are uniquely different from anyone else on the planet. You have unique looks, habits, knowledge, and talents and you are the only person exactly like you. Embrace this.

It's not healthy for humans to compare themselves to other people. In some circumstances, you'll get the idea that you are better than others. This can cause you to become complacent and smug which can lead to laziness and a lack of self-development. You can start to believe in your superiority over other people.

In other situations, you can feel that you fall short or are lacking in some way. This is a false assumption, too. You may merely not have the life experience or information that someone else has. This doesn't make you inferior, it means you have work to do.

You may have had a much more challenging start in life. Maybe you don't have a great support system at home or have had to deal with a poor educational system. It's not fair to hold yourself up against other people that may have had better luck. There's no way to make a reasonable comparison from you to others.

Even within families, each child will have had a completely unique experience being born at a different times.

Parents can change jobs, get divorced, go through things that effect their individual children in different ways. Parents are people too and they can experience different life situations which influence how they care for you and your siblings.

The only positive way to compare yourself to anyone is when you admire other people's achievements or abilities and then model yourself accordingly. You can find out what steps led to their success. You can try to follow in their footsteps and learn from their successes and even their failures. In this way, someone you admire, even if you don't know them personally, can become a mentor and spur you on to do better. Or perhaps, there is one thing about them you would like to emulate, be more like. Perhaps you see a person's kindness toward another person and think, *I'd like to be more kind.* If someone is exceptional at a skill you admire, cooking, playing a sport or instrument, excelling in a school subject like math or science, you can consider how they honed that skill, maybe even ask them for advice or assistance to improve those skills in you.

There are many people you admire that you will likely never meet, but looking at their history, the path they took to get where they are, gives you a roadmap to follow.

So, rather than comparing yourself to others, find your own direction, ask for help along the way and enjoy the journey through school and beyond. Put down any negative baggage you have collected and you will find that you achieve much more, much more quickly as well.

It's not bad to be in friendly competition or wrong to be inspired by someone to go to the next level. It can lead to accomplishing something you never thought possible.

Three Ways to Stop Comparing Yourself to Others

Revel in competition and reject comparison.

There is a big difference between competition and comparison, and it's fairly easily defined. Competition drives you to be the best you can be, and makes you feel positive about yourself.

Comparison makes us feel bad about ourselves from the get-go and either holds us back or gives us a false sense of superiority. I will tell you a secret. No matter how good you are at something, someone will come along who is better than you at that same thing. The same applies to being bad at something. You may think you're the worst at sport or a subject. Trust me, someone is worse than you at it. So, why even think in terms of comparison. It's pointless.

Celebrate other people's success.

There is a great amount of power in celebrating the wins of other people. It reminds you that if it's possible for them, it's possible for you too.

Retrain your brain by shutting down negative talk.

When we start hearing the voice in our head saying, you'll never be as good as someone else, shut it down with positive self-talk.

Try to figure out what's making you start the negative self-talk.

Example: "He gave a terrific presentation. Mine will probably suck."

Flip things around by being positive.

"His presentation was great. Good thing he warmed them up for my talk. I'm excited to explain my opinion!"

Something as simple as being mindful and noticing when negative self-talk is happening will start retraining your brain to stop comparing.

Compliment rather than compare.

Whenever you find you are comparing yourself to someone else, go right up to that person and compliment them on the very thing you're jealous of so you can turn comparison into celebrating. You'll feel good about yourself when you do this.

Focus on your own path.

There is only one you. You were created to do incredible things on earth. The faster you get onto your own path, the sooner you'll feel in tuned. Your unique way of being is of great significance to you because it will allow others to see your special gifts.

Remember, you have a special set of gifts, personality traits, skills and talents that are unique to you.

Using the Technology: Social Media, Texting, and Websites

Ultimately, it's best to try to minimize the time you spend on Social Media where you find yourself buying into false comparisons. Most times you are comparing the messiness of your life to someone's highlight reel.

How many times do you see your friends posting things on social media that make them look better than they really are? Sometimes people share far too much, showing pictures of themselves doing things they shouldn't do, like drinking or partying to make it seem like they're cool or super happy.

Social media gives people the opportunity to "invent" their lives rather than honestly brand themselves. The good news is that, used as a tool, social media can help you create your "brand."

If you enjoy outdoors activities like hiking, swimming, or running, posting pictures of your experiences with these activities can increase your brand.

"Wow, Jan's pictures of the hike she went on look awesome. She certainly enjoys the great outdoors."

If being an "outdoorsy" person is important to you, sharing that information can lead to friends who also enjoy what you do. It can help you be seen as a person to include in certain activities or even lead to a job that you might enjoy.

Sharing ACTUAL accomplishments like winning a swim meet or getting a part in the school play, help define your brand.

Swimmer - Athlete - Actor.

Sharing information about the good works you do, like volunteering at a homeless shelter or hospital, by posting pictures or messages about your experiences lets people see your heart. You are telling the world that there are things you care about and just what those things are.

The bad thing is that the internet is FOREVER. Things you post will always be there. Yes, some platforms like Snap Chat and Tik Tok offer you the opportunity to post something that dissipates within minutes or seconds of posting it. But I hate to tell you that there are people called hackers who can grab those posts before they disappear so even those sites are not "safe."

Texting:

Texting is fine, but if you only text and never learn to speak to people aloud, you lose a lot of the elements of personal communication. You can't hear the inflection in a person's voice when you text. You can't tell if they are mad, sarcastic, sad, serious. A person's voice tells you a lot about how they are feeling or what they are thinking.

Another issue with texting is punctuation and short cuts. Many people feel like they don't need to use punctuation in texting. Without punctuation, meanings can be lost or confused.

Here is an example of text confusion without punctuation:

You have a little fight with a close friend and are texting to try to make things right with them. You ask them to stop by your house to talk and make up.

They text - can't make it work

You think - *Oh, no! They must be so mad they don't think they can make our relationship work.*

What they meant was - Can't make it, work. Meaning: I can't come over right now, I have to work.

See the difference? Texting is fine but it is not perfect. Be cautious as to how you use it and communicate well.

Emojis and texting shorthand don't belong in school or professional communication, particularly in writing. LOL is laughing out loud in text but has no meaning in a written homework assignment. Keep those things to texting only.

And be sure that the people you "shorthand" with know the lingo. One my friend's mom's thought that LOL meant Lots Of Love. She heard that one of her aunts was ill and wrote LOL to her cousin who did not did not see the humor in her mom's illness.

Your Social Media Accounts

What social media do you participate in? Let's consider what each of some of the major ones offer.

Instagram:

Instagram is mostly image and video driven. Be careful that you post images and videos that show you in a good light, that tell people positive things about you. Images are powerful and videos get a lot more attention than text posts most of the time.

Do your Instagram pictures tell people who you are? Are they improving or hurting your brand.

LinkedIn:

Have you ever looked at LinkedIn? LinkedIn is for business. People use LinkedIn to meet other businesspeople, to learn new things and read interesting articles, to get a job or hire new people, and to share information about their businesses and the businesses they work with.

It might seem silly for you to create a LinkedIn profile while you're in high school, but actually, it's the smartest thing you can do regardless of what kind of career you choose. Colleges will look at your social media profiles when you apply and if you show that you are invested in the topics that matter in the career you're considering, that you've connected with influencers and leaders in the field, you are heads and shoulders above other candidates.

There are groups for everything from architecture to playwriting on LinkedIn. There are so many types of interests being considered and written about. Connecting with other people that share your interests could lead to mentors or help you connect with people who can advance your career and shape your future. It's a very powerful platform but you must be at least 16 years-old to create the account.

You Tube:

There is likely to be a video on anything you ever want to learn about on You Tube. How to videos, music, movies, all sorts of things are on that platform. Unless you are teaching something or want to share something like your music or some other talent you have with the world, you are not likely to create a You Tube Channel. However, it's a powerful tool and a much-used social media platform.

Snapchat and Tik Tok:

Sites like Snapchat and Tik Tok are fun to play on. They offer the opportunity to post pictures and messages that are usually only available for a short time before they become inaccessible. They don't have lasting value, but they may not just disappear the way you think they do. Hackers can grab anything and keep hold of it.

Pinterest:

Pinterest is great tool for finding interesting things like recipes, décor, and fashion ideas and all kinds of visual art. If you're an artist, crafter, photographers, cook or can share images that help you share your ideas and talents, Pinterest can be very helpful as a brand builder.

Facebook:

You may not use Facebook because it tends to be used by people over 30 and even your parents and grandparents might have active accounts there. Facebook has a business component too. Lots of business use Facebook to promote their companies and events they are involved in. Facebook live has become a way to educate people, especially about a person's work with presentations to teach people about their services and products.

If you start a little business, or want to get part-time work after school, Facebook might be a way to promote yourself in a positive way. By posting that you are willing to mow lawns or that you make something like jewelry or cupcakes, you can spread the word about your business endeavors. This too is part of your "brand."

Handyperson – Artist – Baker – person who is ambitious and willing to work for their money. These things tell people who you are.

Just remember, if you are on any social media platform, everything you post there is there **FOREVER.** If you post that you are skipping school and post pictures of yourself at the beach, your teachers and school administrators are very likely to see that. The same applies later in life if you skip work for the day. Bosses are on social media too.

If you post images and positive messages about good things you're doing, that will follow you as well.

Creating a Website

Here is something many people don't know. Someday, you may want to build a website to help you market yourself and secure your brand. Owning the domain name of your own name is a smart thing to do if it's possible. If your name is John Smith, it's not likely that you can buy Johnsmith.com. That is likely taken.

However, let's say you have an interest in something like golf. You can make a simple website and name it something like, JohnSmithGolf-Lover.com. There are lots of free or cheap website builder sites like WordPress, WIX, or Squarespace that allow you to make your own website and sharing the things that interest you. It's fun and an excellent skill to begin to hone. You can post pictures and write blogs, find articles to post and promote your website on your social media sites.

If you want people to know what you are interested in and learn more about you, starting a small website with the help of your parents, or a teacher or even friends, can be a great way to begin to shape your identity and increase your brand.

But first, you must begin to work out what matters to you, what interests you, what makes you happy. Your words matter. The images you put out into the world matter. Don't kid yourself that just because there are so many posts, pictures, and videos flying by on social media that no one will notice if you post something that will be embarrassing or damaging to you later that it will get lost.

Begin to realize that you can use social media in very powerful ways to make your mark on the world and create a real brand that lets the world know who you are and what you stand for.

Start early. Be ahead of the herd!

Chapter 4 Exercises:

What social media do you use?

How do you use those platforms?

Research domain names. There are many places where you can buy a domain name for less than $15 (often a lot less). See if your own name is available. If you have an unusual name it might be, and you can ask your parents if you can buy that domain name for future reference. If you are tech savvy, you might want to start a website and share your talents or write blogs about what you are interested in.

If you are 16 or older, sign up for LinkedIn and create an account. If you are younger than 16, work with your parents to start an account. Find three groups on LinkedIn that share some interest of yours. Begin to connect with people that share those interests. Always keep your parents and mentors aware of your social media interactions to help guide you and keep you safe.

Accelerate

MINDSET, LEARNABILITY, TALENTS, AND SKILLS

THE STORY OF TWO HARRYS

Harry 1 has always loved the water. Even though he grew up in rural Kansas, he seemed to enjoy swimming more than any other activity and spent all his free time at the local YMCA. His parents realized this was going to be a big part of his life. They asked him if he wanted swimming lessons and he was very happy to work with instructors and trainers. He began competing in swimming and diving in competitions in 5th grade and he won most of his meets. He found that he liked to practice in the early morning before school so by 8th grade he was getting up at 5 am nearly every day to get to the pool where he trained alone. He did so all through high school and Harry got a scholarship to Stanford University, the number one college in the country for men's competition swimming. By his junior year in college he was invited to try out for the Olympic swim team and made it. He won two gold medals and a bronze medal for his efforts with the United States Swim team in his individual races.

Harry 2 grew up in a family who loved the water so much that they chose to live in Florida where they could be around water nearly all year round. Harry was swimming before he walked. He learned to swim when his father tossed him off the boat, laughing as he paddled wildly until he finally got the hang of it. In a few hours, he was jumping in on his own and swimming back and forth to his two older brothers. When he got to high school, the coach of the swim team spoke at orientation. He was seeking new recruits for the team and, on a lark, Harry signed up. At first, his swimming technique was raw, and his form was poor. He nearly quit in anger when he wasn't the best swimmer in the freshman group. But the coach saw something in him and talked him into staying. He worked with him one on one after school for weeks and soon Harry was out-swimming many of the seniors. Harry practiced two afternoons a week and almost every Saturday morning with two of his teammates.

Harry 2 found he was more motivated to swim better when he was swimming with other swimmers and having fun. He needed the camaraderie and competition. By his Junior year in High School, Harry started taking his swimming more seriously. In college, he continued to compete and practice and realized he was best as the anchor on relay races. He tried out and was able to join the United State Olympic swim team and he and his teammates won gold in two relay competitions.

Learnability and 21st Century Skills

What is the path to learning in the 21st-century?

There are 6 steps that are considered to be the path to the way we learn.

1. Identify what you want to learn
2. Know how you would prefer to learn it
3. Create pathways to your learning
4. Assess where you are in your learning process
5. Produce evidence of what you've learned

6. Improve and iterate on what you've learned

Rinse and repeat! Learning is a forever process. Doing this will continually strengthen your brain.

Sometimes we figure out early in life what our path will be. Remember the story of the two Thomases from Chapter One? Thomas 2 had a life changing experience that led to his desire to become a doctor. He had a strong inclination to take this path and took steps toward his goal very early on.

For many of us, we have no idea what we want to be or what our best skills and paths could lead us to. Sometimes, like with the story of Harry Two in this chapter, it takes more time.

There are people who have done many years of research to help us figure out what our best paths might be; what skills might best lead us to a career.

The High 5 Test

I want you to go to the website below and take this free test; the High 5 Test. This test was created to help people discover what they're naturally good at. Over a million people have taken it.

https://high5test.com/ 100 questions and free to take!

HIGH5 strengths are recurring patterns of thoughts, decisions, actions, and feelings that satisfy 5 major criteria:

1. You feel natural at using and developing your ability;

2. You get positive energy when using your strengths;

3. Others also perceive it as your strength;

4. It goes along with your values and understanding of a strength;

5. It satisfies your inner needs.

Unless you were raised on a desert island, you grew up around other people and have learned to socialize and you have input from others and the world/environment in which you grew up and live. Some of your strengths will be dependent on the culture in which you grew up. What's seen as a strength in one society might not line up with the values of another group of people. So, when considering what you're good at, what your strengths are, your environment, culture, or community might not see that as a strength.

Strengths can't be cultivated easily in a place that doesn't make sense. In the case of Harry one, he had to really love swimming. He wasn't surrounded by water in warm weather like Harry two. He had to really want it and make it fit in his environment. Harry two grew up with water and swimming being a regular part of his life and due to where he grew up.

It might be very difficult to become a cross country skier if you live in the desert. If you grow up in a religion that doesn't allow dancing, ballerina might be a tough career to aspire to. Going against the grain to achieve greatness is difficult, but not impossible. But it's easier when those 5 criteria points above fall into place.

Let's consider how the two Harry's line up with those 5 criteria that the High 5 test believe matters.

1. Both of them had a natural affinity for swimming.
2. Both got positive energy from swimming.
3. Others saw them as being strong swimmers and competitors.
4. Swimming represented a positive value.
5. Swimming met an inner need for each of them though perhaps a slightly different need.

Mindset: Openness to Learning

"I think anything is possible if you have the mindset and the will and desire to do it and put the time in." - Roger Clemens

What is your Mindset toward learning? Do you enjoy learning new things or is it a big chore?

We all enjoy the feeling of being good at something, but it takes time, information and often practice, to become good at something.

Harry 1 learned early on that he really enjoyed swimming. He like to glide through the water in the pool in the early hours of the morning with no other sound than the swish of his arms and legs moving swiftly and perfectly. He liked winning. He liked doing that solo.

Harry 2 preferred to practice in a group. He was learning to swim by watching others and enjoying their company. For him, it was a team effort, not a solo flight.

When we begin to get good at something, it's more fun, isn't it? But sometimes we quit trying when the skill doesn't come easily.

How do you like to study?

Do you like to study alone in a quiet room? Do you prefer to study with other people in a group setting?

Some people can only learn with the TV on for mindless noise in the background. Other people need to have complete silence.

When it comes to cultivating intelligence, mindset is a huge factor. The beliefs you have about yourself and your basic qualities matter. If you don't believe you can be a genius, then you may not be able to become one. But if you open your mind to the possibility, then your future becomes an unwritten book.

Students who aren't encouraged to believe in their own abilities may never progress in subject areas that they don't already feel inclined toward. Students who are encouraged to believe in their own intelligence are better positioned to become the next Einstein. This quality of openness and curiosity is generally present in people we would call geniuses.

Human intelligence is malleable, meaning it can be changed through exposure to new information or even by looking at what you already know in a new way. There's no limit to how much you can learn. No one's brain has ever been filled.

The brain continually changes by making new neuroconnections between its cells, which represent new knowledge or skills, and when this happens, we say someone has become smarter. It's possible for humans to become smarter all the time and in any area of study.

Some subjects will be harder for you to learn than others but learning in any area is possible. Intelligence is not a fixed quantity that you got at birth and are stuck with. You become smarter every day, and the intelligence you achieve in your lifetime is unknowable. That said, it does appear that your *mindset* about learning will have a heavy impact on how much you will learn and just about everything else in your life.

"With a fixed mindset, you believe you are who you are and you cannot change. This creates problems when you're challenged because anything that appears to be more than you can handle is bound to make you feel hopeless and overwhelmed."

- Travis Bradberry

Your mindset is your view about your own intelligence and abilities. This view affects your willingness to engage in learning tasks and how much, if any, effort you are willing to expend to meet a learning challenge.

Mindset - Dweck's Theory

Carol Dweck is a Psychologist who is a pioneer in the study of human motivation. She is perhaps best-known for her research on how *mindsets* influence motivation and success.

Dweck has spent more than 30 years researching the mindsets of learners and how mindset affects a person's view of their intelligence.

She believes that mindsets fall into two categories: fixed mindsets and growth mindsets.

A person with a fixed mindset believes that intelligence is a fixed trait despite hundreds of studies that have found otherwise.

If your mindset is fixed you believe that either you're smart in a given area/subject or you're not; there is nothing you can do to improve in that area. Individuals with fixed mindsets believe their intelligence is reflected in their academic performance. If a student doesn't do well in a class, it's because he or she is not "smart" in that subject area.

Individuals with fixed mindsets mistakenly believe they shouldn't need to work hard to do well because the smart students don't have to. However, when researchers asked students who consistently achieved high grades about their work, they reported working very hard at academic studies. Conversely, people with fixed mindsets believe that putting in the effort won't make any difference in the outcome *("I'm just not good at math and no matter how hard I try, I never will be!")*. They falsely come to the conclusion that learning comes easy to the students at the top of the class, and that they were born that way.

In contrast to that, people with growth mindsets believe that intelligence grows as you add new knowledge and skills. Those with growth mindsets value hard work, learning, and challenges and see failure as a message that they need to change something in order to succeed the next time.

Thomas Edison is reported to have tried hundreds of times before he got the lightbulb to work. At one point, he was asked by a New York Times reporter about all his failures and whether he was going to give up. Edison responded, "I have not failed 700 times. I've succeeded in proving 700 ways how not to build a light bulb" (as cited in Ferlazzo, 2011).

Shortly after that interview he was successful in getting the light bulb to work. We've all benefited from his growth mindset. Individuals with growth mindsets are willing to take learning risks and understand that through practice and effort (sometimes a lot of effort) their abilities can improve. Those with growth mindsets believe that their brains are malleable, that intelligence and abilities constantly grow, and that only time will tell how smart they can become.

The significance of Dweck's research for high school students is profound. Each fall, tens of thousands of students enroll in classes that they believe they don't have the ability to pass. They also believe that hiring a tutor, visiting the teacher during office hours for extra help, or even working harder will make no difference. They hold this belief because they have a fixed mindset in that area.

The next time you take a class on a subject you're a little afraid to tackle because you think you are not "smart" in that area, keep in mind that practice can make a huge difference in your learning success. The class may not be easy for you, but if you take the time to expand your knowledge by researching the topic or accepting help like tutoring, and if you work hard (keep a growth mindset), there is no telling what you will achieve. Today's student has the advantage of the internet. There is so much information to be found if you look. There are videos to watch, articles to read, blogs about almost every subject. Don't be afraid to ask for help. Dig in and do the work and you can learn anything. It'll expand your mind and your intelligence.

Fixed Mindsets and Laziness

High school and college teachers often see lack of effort as laziness. If you won't make the effort to ask for help or do some personal extra research, ask yourself why.

Students with fixed mindsets believe extra work is just a wasted effort. Even if they try to work hard, they tell themselves, "This is hard.... I can't get it.... Maybe I should drop the class." Studying with that attitude is not productive at all.

In contrast, those with growth mindsets work hard even for classes they don't like, and because they know the effort will likely produce improved results, they see greater success.

Those students aren't smarter; they just see themselves differently.

Changing to a Growth Mindset

Nearly everyone has a fixed mindset about something, but there are things you can do to change your fixed mindsets into growth mindsets.

Dweck's research found that students of all ages, from early grade school through college, can learn to have growth mindsets. It is important to recognize that your intellectual skills can be cultivated through hard work, reading, education, the confrontation of challenges, and other activities. Students may know how to study, but they won't want to if they believe that their efforts are futile.

If you accept that effort will pay dividends then you're on your way to greater academic and life success. I'm not going to lie and tell you that you're going to enjoy every subject you will be tasked to study, only that everyone can improve in academic areas. Even your teacher was a novice at one time and had to spend a good deal of time studying in order to become an expert in his or her field.

When you focus on how you can improve, by finding a new strategy, getting a study partner, reviewing on a daily basis, or putting in more time and effort, you can discover how to overcome the failure. Your ability to face a challenge is not dependent on your actual skills or abilities; it's based on the mindset you bring to the challenge. You need to be willing to take learning risks and be open to learning all you can from your experiences. This message can be difficult to accept, but it is crucial to your growth and development as a learner.

Your performance reflects only your current skills and efforts, not your intelligence, worth, or potential. Improvement in yoga comes solely from improved technique and increased effort. The more you practice and the better your technique becomes, the better you get and the easier it becomes. Being a weakling is simply a current state of performance, not who you are. High school classes are often like weight lifting. You start small, and with repeated practice, you keep building brain muscle.

How to Help Yourself

The way you help yourself is to use self-talk. Carol Dweck offers the following suggestions:

Step 1. You need to learn to hear your fixed mindset "voice." Students can learn to listen and recognize when they are engaging in a fixed mindset. Students may say to themselves or hear in their head things like, "Are you sure you can do it? Maybe you don't have the talent," or, "What if you fail? You'll be a failure." Also, catch yourself exaggerating the situation, as that can signal a fixed mindset.

For example, you might think you can't do math but while geometry, algebra, or calculus might be challenging, it's difficult to believe a high school student can't do any math.

A person with a fixed mindset will say things like, "I can't give presentations." This is a lie that person is telling themselves to explain the fear of standing up in front of a group. Nearly everyone has a similar fear but when you hear that little voice in your head saying, "You're going to mess up and make a fool of yourself," you have to tell that voice to shush!

If you think of it like a devil one shoulder whispering in your ear that you're going to fail, you have to imagine an angel on the other shoulder, telling you, "You've got this!"

Step 2. You need to recognize you have a choice. How you interpret challenges, setbacks, and criticism is a choice. You need to know you can choose to ramp up your strategies and effort, stretch yourself, and expand your abilities. It's up to you.

Step 3. You need to talk back to yourself with a growth mindset. THE FIXED MINDSET says, "Are you sure you can do it? Maybe you don't have the talent." THE GROWTH MINDSET answers, "I'm not sure I can do it now, but I can learn to do it." FIXED MINDSET: "What if you fail-you'll be a failure." GROWTH MINDSET: "Most successful people had failures along the way."

Step 4. Students need to take growth mindset action. The more you choose the growth mindset voice, the easier it will become to choose it again and again.

Chapter 5 Exercises:

There are three basic types of learning: Visual, Auditory, and Kinesthetic.

It's important to identify the way you absorb information best. Some people need to see information. This means they will likely learn by reading or watching demonstrations. Some need to hear the information. Books on tape, lectures, work best for them. Others are kinesthetic learners meaning they learn by doing.

Do you know what your best way or ways of learning are? Once you figure that out, you will save a lot of time and effort when studying and choosing classes that suit your learning skills.

How do you learn best?

- By reading?
- By listening to someone talk – teacher lectures?

- By watching videos?
- Alone or in a group?
- In class, at a library or at home?
- What other factors help or hinder your ability to learn? Ex. noise, where you sit etc.

Do you learn in one or more of these ways?

- Experiential (by experiencing things)
- Visually
- Auditory

- **What can you do to improve your mindset about a subject you don't like or think you are good at?**
- **Find someone that is struggling with a subject you are really good at. Offer to help them improve.**

Extra exercise for students already in or entering high school:

Research colleges that offer subject majors that you think you're good at and like.

"You are the average of the five people you spend the most time with, including yourself."

- Celestine Chua

6

THE THREE R'S: RELATIONSHIPS, RELATIONSHIPS, AND RELATIONSHIPS

THE DEFINITION OF NETWORKING:

- *The action or process of interacting with others to exchange information and develop professional or social contacts.*
- *"The skills of networking, bargaining, and negotiation."*

Note: Computer networking refers to linking multiple devices so that they can readily share information and software resources; not unlike the way people network to share information and resources.

Networking is the exchange of information and ideas among people with a common profession or special interest, usually in an informal social setting. People often network with one another to share ideas, learn about one another's businesses in order to refer one another or make use of one another services.

In every city in America, every day of the work week, there are breakfast, lunch, and after work networking meetings where like-minded professionals get together to discuss their business dealings and share information.

There are websites and groups, both local and international that people can join.

You've experienced this to some degree in your life already. You may attend a church, belong to a choir, perhaps you've joined a club, or you've played on a team sport. Whenever and wherever people gather together with common interests, a form of networking happens.

We learn about the people in the group. We call upon them for assistance or meet with them socially. We ask them for help learning a new skill or ask them if they can refer us to someone who can offer a skill they don't have but whom they can recommend.

If your mom or dad needs to hire a plumber or a new mechanic, they are likely to ask someone they know well and trust for a "referral." They want a recommendation for someone that person trusts so therefore mom or dad might be able to trust as well. That's a form of networking.

You hopefully have a circle of trusted friends. As you get older, this circle becomes very important. They're part of your "network." They know other people or meet other people who they bring into the circle. Each person in the circle brings their individual talents and ideas, their personality and assets. If someone in your network is great at math, he or she might be the person that helps you improve your math skills. Someone will get a driver's license and a car first. That person will likely be the one to take the others to the mall, the movies, or drive to and from school.

You can create all kinds of networks and connections as you grow. You will begin to see what interests you and you'll find groups of people to connect with through those interests.

Social Media platforms have lots of special interest groups. Writers, artists, realtors, every profession, has groups that people interested in those topics can find and join.

Meetup.com offers a variety of groups to join, some that meet in person, some that share ideas virtually.

In high school, there are always clubs and organizations you can join. Sports teams will require tryouts, drama clubs will hold auditions, but many clubs are just fun to belong to and require nothing more than genuine interest and time commitment. Find your tribe, the people that you want to share information and resources with, who can refer to others, learn from, get referrals from. Those groups, the people in them, will be tremendous assets in your academic life and will often carry into your adult life. These "networks" will be there to help you.

Don't be afraid to ask people to help; be clear on what you want.

Seeking Mentors

What is a mentor:

A mentor is someone who teaches, guides, and lifts you up by virtue of his or her experience and insight. They're usually someone a little farther ahead of you on the path—though that doesn't always mean they're older! A mentor is someone with a head full of experience and heart full of generosity that brings those things together in your life. – Dr. John Maxwell – renowned author/speaker.

Mentors can be a parent or grandparent or even a sibling. They can be a trusted friend or a total stranger who believes in helping others, lifting others up and sharing their wisdom, knowledge, talents, and experiences. Mentors can fast track you to a place it might take much longer to reach than without them. Mentors can show you where the pitfalls are, where not to go as much as where to go. You get to hear the stories of their successes but also their failures. I think most mentors will tell you that their failures taught them a great deal more than their successes did.

Be prepared:

If you seek out a mentor who is willing to help you, prepare for the times you will meet with him or her. Have questions, bring a notebook, and take notes. Be respectful and be on TIME! Don't miss meetings or make them wait for you. Remember the story of the two Thomases? Thomas two found a doctor to mentor him. The doctor was much older and was excited to see a young man who wanted to follow in his footsteps. True mentors WANT to help you. They want to see you succeed. They often hope you will be able to take their place someday and hope that you will be an even bigger success than they are. Teachers want you to learn everything they know and then go beyond that.

Do teachers realize when they are teaching a student who later becomes President of the United States? No! Could those people have become president without their teachers? Hard No! Do you think teachers are jealous of the success of a student that excels to that degree, or are they proud of the part they played in that person's rise to the most powerful person on earth? I'm guessing having taught a future president would be a point of pride for most if not all of them.

"I taught that person!" What a proud thing to be able to say.

So, don't think that mentors are mad at you or bothered by you. If they agree to mentor you it's because they want to see you succeed and maybe even share in your success. They will be proud of you.

How do I find a mentor?

Mentors are everywhere. If there's a teacher, coach, pastor, family friend or relative that you think might be a good mentor, buck up and ask them. Don't let shyness or laziness or any other block you've created in your head stop you. If they say no, then thank them politely and look for someone else. You will find the right mentor if you do the work.

Some you may never meet but you may follow their blog or their twitter feed. Some you may hear speak. Start by considering who you see as successful in an area or subject you want to learn about or might see as your future career like Thomas did with the doctor. How can you access that person? You may read his or her books or blogs, follow them on social media. You might be able to connect with them through those social media accounts. Make a short video or write a heartfelt note and tell the mentor that seems unreachable how much their books and blogs move you. Message them, write them from their websites. Ask for their help. They might turn you down, but they might surprise you. What do you have to lose by asking? So, ASK!

Getting Ahead of the Competition

LinkedIn means business:

You will be head and shoulders ahead of most high school students and even many college students if you create a LinkedIn account and participate on that platform. The average yearly income of the people who have LinkedIn accounts is more than $75,000 per year. These are successful, serious businesspeople. And don't think it's just things like accounting, finance, and law. There are entire groups dedicated to art, science, theater, playwriting, fiction writing, you name it. These are people who take what they do seriously. They want to connect with like-minded people, people who want to help each other grow and succeed. There will be great articles to read about everything from business to politics to art. Check in on LinkedIn at least a few times a week. Join groups, connect with people with similar likes and interests. You will very likely find mentors there even if it's a matter of people you follow and pay attention to whose posts and articles teach you something. An important tip: fill out your LinkedIn profile as completely as possible. Don't just put your name and a few little details. If you need help filling that out, ask your parents or teachers to help you. The more people know about your interests, your hopes for your future education and career choices, the more you will see people reach out to try to help you. I'll tell you a secret. Older people LOVE when younger people show interest in their careers, subject matter, and interests. It makes us proud and happy when you SEE us as viable and knowledgeable and most of us will fall all over ourselves to help you. If you think you want to be a salesperson, realtor, business owner, coach, artist, writer or almost anything, reaching out to people in those careers will get you far more response than you would imagine and LinkedIn is where many of those people hang out.

Volunteering:

One of the best things you can do to learn and grow is to volunteer. There are so many opportunities to volunteer at hospitals and churches and of course food pantries and places that feed the homeless. Many volunteer positions won't relate in any way to your career choices or interests, but you will meet people who have the same heart that you have. You will meet people from all walks of life that want to help others and some of those people will become friends, mentors, and leaders in your life. Some you may help mentor yourself. Helping others has far reaching benefits that aren't always initially seen but the connections you make, the people who you touch, and the people who see your good intentions and strong morals and heart, will affect your life and your future more than you can imagine.

Internships:

Many companies seek interns. Go to your school counsellor and ask if he or she can look into internship availabilities for you. Marketing companies, law firms, architects, and many types of businesses will seek interns. Interns are free labor. I'm not going to lie to you. However, becoming an intern at a business is invaluable for you. You will get to rub elbows with people who are working in the field you're interested in. You'll get to see what the daily work and life of these people consists of. You may learn that you LOVE this work. You may learn that you HATE it.

If you think you want to be a graphic artist or website designer, a marketing company may let you play with the software and learn to do some of the simple tasks they have on their plate. They will likely show you some tricks and short cuts. You may get to answer phones and you will likely run errands. It will be fun, if you allow yourself to be open to new experiences and aren't afraid to ask for help.

Internships can turn into paid jobs, summer employment or even a position that is promised to you when you complete your education. Your internship will likely offer you some mentorship.

The main thing is you will get real life experience in that field. It will let you see how the real world works and what professionals in that field do on the daily. Nothing could be better.

To seek internships, try Indeed.com. There are often internships listed there and sometimes there are some that even offer a little pay for your efforts.

Hang out with people you want to be like:

Whenever it's possible, surround yourself with people you admire and want to be like. Don't waste your time with people who are negative and will bring you down. Find people who have the same heart and mindset you do. This is where volunteering and internships can help. If you have friends who are always down, always complaining, never study and show little to no ambition, try to help them improve their outlook. Try to find out why they are so negative and why they have a fixed mindset. Do your best to help them move into a growth mindset but if you fail at that, spend less time with them. Spend more time with uplifting people, people with growth mindsets and interests that match yours. Reach up, not down.

Chapter 6 Exercises:

Name 5 people living you wish you could talk to about your future. This can be realistic or as far-fetched as possible.

1. _____
2. _____
3. _____
4. _____
5. _____

What kinds of questions would you ask each of them?

_____

_____

_____

_____

Think about 5 people in your life that you can reach out to and ask to mentor you. You only need one to say yes.

Seek one thing you can volunteer for that will help others and get involved.

Look for internships that might fit your interests and if it's possible, apply for a few.

DISTRACTION IS YOUR ONLY COMPETITION

FOCUS IS OUT OF FOCUS

I've been thinking a lot about the difference between a student that is successful in school and one that is not.

So, in doing research, I came across two principles in *The Princeton Review* book that I wholeheartedly agree with based on my experiences working with students in schools. The first point, referred to as the real secret between a smart student and other students, is ***attitude***.

Attitude is the way you see and interpret your experiences. It's the sum total of your beliefs, expectations, and values. It's the way you determine meaning or the importance of an event or your response to it.

The second point references being a smart student and how smart students do things differently. ***Smart students have different skills, goals, habits, priorities and strategies because they see school, the learning process, and even themselves differently***. Being a smart student means taking charge and teaching yourself. Becoming a smart student means taking responsibility for your education. ***No school can teach you the way you learn best, so how much you learn and how well you do is up to you.***

My third point is "Focus is out of Focus." You may be wondering what that means so I'll explain it this way. No one teaches you how to use your mind. There's no manual on how to use your mind.

When you purchase a blender, a car, most anything, operating instructions come with it. Even our iPhones come with a manual. Ask yourself this question:

What will happen if you practice the same thing 8 to 10 hours a day? Day in and day out, over and over again week in and week out, 365 days a year?

You would get really good at that thing because you practiced it consistently.

Think about your day — today!

Outsourcing Your Brain to Your Personal Device

We practice ourselves into distraction. We are constantly picking up our phone when it dings. While doing homework, most people are viewing IG stories or snaps on their iPhones. While eating, most people are viewing their phone screens watching Tik Tok videos, YouTube clips, or memes.

Your *AWARENESS* is moving from one thing to another, which is the classic definition of DISTRACTION, which has the opposite meaning of **FOCUS/CONCENTRATION**. Ultimately we have become very good at being distracted because it's what we are practicing day in and day out.

We spend so much time on phones, computers, playing video games, watching videos, or texting, we can't focus on anything for more than a few minutes if not seconds.

When we do this, we are outsourcing our brains to our personal devices. We become very dependent on these devices, particularly our phones. Many people cannot walk away from their phones for more than a few minutes without feeling panicked. If you are experiencing that feeling, we will have some exercises to help with that. We distract ourselves and diminish our abilities to concentrate.

When I ask parents, teachers, and adults who have children in their lives - "Have you taught your child or student how to concentrate?"

Every parent and teacher I asked had the same answer — **NO!**

I asked students:

- Has anyone ever taught you how to focus or concentrate?
- Did your parents or a teacher teach you that skill?

They replied NO, however some students added that they had experienced the feeling of focus or concentration while playing an instrument, being involved in drama, or playing a sport. How ironic! We ask students to focus or concentrate, yet we do not teach students how to concentrate or focus.

Getting in the Zone

Focus is a life skill and one that has served me well in my athletic days and in life. In sports we call it being in *"**THE ZONE**."* Being in THE ZONE is special, it's a time when things just go great.

You see that pitch being thrown in softball, you see the play before it happens in soccer, football, or volleyball. It's just a time when you are at a heightened sense of awareness.

You may have experienced that feeling of THE ZONE, but never thought about how to apply it to learning in school or your daily life outside of school. Getting into THE ZONE requires practice. Musicians, athletes, actresses/actors practice their craft. They will spend hours upon hours of time day in and day out practicing their skills. Think about the breakout Grammy Award winner Billie Eilish or Lizzo, or soccer great Megan Rapinoe, or the super talented cellist Yo-Yo Ma, or tennis great Serena Williams, or the late Kobe Bryant. These talented individuals spent great lengths practicing year after year to get better.

So, here is $10,000 question —

How do you get better at concentration?

Simply —

You start by *focusing on one thing a time* and the best way to <u>get better</u> at concentration is by *integrating the practice into your life!*

. . .

Here are a few examples:

For example, when talking with someone in person, make eye contact with them and give them your full attention. Put all your devices away and just focus on the exchange of information between you both. When listening, listen with the intention of understanding, which is the level of empathetic listening and or active listening. Do not listen with the intent of responding or finishing one's sentence. Don't try to think of what you're going to say once they stop talking.

Another example - set a timer for 25 minutes and put your mobile device away while doing work. Gradually build up more time away from your device as you go about your day.

Here is a method you can use to help you. It's called, the Pomodoro method.

The inventor named his system "**Pomodoro**" after the tomato-shaped **timer** he used to track his work and time when he was in college. The idea is simple: When you have to tackle any larger task or series of tasks, work in short, timed intervals ("Pomodoros") that are spaced out by short breaks. This can also work for trying to train yourself to focus.

You can choose either a 5- or 15-minute break from the work or use the "break" as free time to check email, texts, memes, social media, etc. Better than doing that is stretching, walking, getting a healthy snack. Learn to dismiss your device on these breaks as often as possible.

Here are links to a couple of those timers:

https://pomofocus.io/

https://tomato-timer.com/

. . .

Chapter 7 Exercises:

Make an intention to learn self-awareness about distraction and time sucks.

Get a small notebook and a pen or pencil and keep it with you for a whole day from the time you rise till you are about to fall asleep. Note the time when you get up and the time when you get in bed to go to sleep when all devices are put away.

- Every time you look at your phone during those hours, make a tick mark on a page in the book and mark the time you picked the phone up and the time you put it down.
- Every time you play a video game, mark the time you start and stop.
- Every time you play around on any social media platform on laptop or phone, mark the time you start and stop.

The next day, count up the minutes and hours you noted and subtract that number from the total number of hours you were awake. Do the math to see the percentage of your waking hours that you were distracting yourself. Ask your parents and friends to try this exercise too. I think it will be enlightening for a lot of people.

Next, get out that same notebook and a pen or pencil and keep it with you for a whole day from the time you rise till you are about to fall asleep. This time, write down every single thing you do from morning till night, what time you started and stopped each activity. It won't be easy so make a game of it. Challenge yourself to keep up with it ALL DAY.

I promise you; these two activities can be life changing.

Accelerate

VALUES AND THE WORD VALUABLE

THE STORY OF TWO TANYAS

Tanya 1 is a freshman in high school. She has a best friend who she says she really values and loves and who she's been friends with since second grade. But her friend doesn't have very good taste in clothing, hair, and make-up. In fact, her friend is often laughed at behind her back because her clothes make her look sloppy and unkempt.

Now that they're in a brand-new school, Tanya wants to fit in, and she is often embarrassed to be seen in public with her friend. She knows that because she is friends with this girl, she is losing opportunities to be invited to parties or to be part of the inner circles of some of the other more well-dressed and well-groomed girls in their school. High school can be difficult, and Tanya wants her friend to be accepted but she wants to be accepted even more. She knows her friend comes from a family that can't afford to buy her nice clothes and make-up. So, Tanya decides to begin to separate herself from her long-time friend.

One day, in the hall after school, a group of girls gang up on Tanya's friend. They make fun of her clothes and hair and call her names. Instead of sticking up for her friend, Tanya joins them and stands their laughing with the other mean girls. Tanya's friend runs off crying and they never speak again. Tanya 1 made a decision about what she values, what her values are, and what was more valuable to her and she chose popularity over friendship.

Tanya 2 is a freshman in high school. She has a best friend who she really values and loves and who she's been friends with since second grade. But her friend doesn't have very good taste in clothing, hair, and make-up. In fact, her friend is often laughed at behind her back because her clothes make her look sloppy and unkempt. Now that they're in a brand-new school, Tanya wants to fit in, and she wants her friend to have a good high school experience as well.

Tanya knows that high school can be rough at times and that kids aren't always nice.

She invites her friend over to her house for a weekend sleepover and she asks her mother to take them to the Goodwill. She knows her friend doesn't come from a wealthy family, so she asks her mom for $20 to buy some things at the thrift store. She makes a fun outing of shopping with her old pal. She gets her to try on some new clothes that are not her usual style. She compliments her on how good she looks and says that she is sharing a gift she got and is buying them both some new things. Tanya 2 has a good eye for clothes and fashion. With just $20 she buys two new outfits for her friend and a hat and blouse for herself.

When they get home, she asks her older sister to help them have a makeover night. With lots of laughter and snacks, they spend the night trying new hairdos and make-up. By the time the night is over, Tanya's longtime friend has a new more fashionable style. "Look how great you look," she tells her. Her friend beams.

Back at school, some mean girls are snickering in the hall after school. They notice Tanya and her friend and are muttering about the change in clothes and hair. Tanya 2 takes her friend's arm and walks proudly past the mean girls with a broad smile. She chose friendship and she knows what is valuable to her.

Knowing Your Values

Knowing your values, your value/worth, and what valuable means in terms of relationships

One of the most important things in life is to know your values. What matters to you, what you value, will shape every other aspect of your life. Tanya one valued acceptance. She did not value true friendship as much as fitting in with people she thought were important. She valued the opinion of the group of girls who thought they were better than her friend over that lifelong friendship. She hurt her friend and gave up someone who was important to her and who likely cared about her a great deal; probably a great deal more than the girls who were making fun of her friend.

Tanya two valued friendship. She found a way to help her friend to navigate some of the, often painful, waters of high school. Even if her friend never dressed or acted like some of the "popular" girls, it is unlikely that she would have given her up for them.

A very important thing to note, she found a way to be honest with kindness instead of cruelty. She didn't have to say something harsh like, "You really need to dress better. We need to get you new clothes and a new look." She, in fact, didn't have to say anything. She used positive actions instead of hurtful words. She used affirmations like, "wow, that outfit looks great on you."

Compliments don't cost anything. Cruelty comes with a *very high price*.

Part of values means knowing your own worth; knowing that you are very valuable regardless of what you look like, dress like, where you come from, how much money you have, or how smart you are. Knowing that you are a valuable person will help you see the value, the worth, of other people and things.

What's important to you?

- Friendship
- Money
- Status
- Being liked/loved
- Being accepted
- Being smart
- Being funny
- Being true to yourself
- Your family
- The earth
- The environment

Once you establish what matters to you most, you can frame your life around that. Like the two Thomases, you can decide why you want a certain career. Do you want to be a doctor or lawyer because those are jobs that pay very well or because those are careers that offer the opportunity to help others.

Do you want to be a teacher because you want summers and week-ends off or because you want to help students learn and grow. In case you aren't aware of this, teachers don't get the "big bucks." You might want to think about your teachers as people. They are working very hard to help you become the best you can be. They are often underappreciated and underpaid. Most of them value you. They value education and what it can do for young people.

You will make so many choices in your life. You will pick friends, colleges, courses of study, careers, life partners, where to live, even mundane things like what to eat for dinner and where to go on vacation. Does it surprise you to know that every single choice you make will be shaped by your values? Yes, even the clothes you wear and what you'll eat for lunch.

Enemies, Frenemies, Alliances/Allies, and Friends

What do each of these words really mean?

Enemy:

An enemy is someone who sets about to undermine you. This person, for whatever reason, wants to see you fail. This can often come from jealousy. A person who sees you succeeding where they are failing is likely to take their own failures out on you. Sometimes we consider people our enemy because our friends, parents, even our country tells us to consider them as such. You may someday read about Romeo and Juliet. Shakespeare wrote about these star-crossed lovers whose two families were sworn enemies. The children of these families adhered to this idea until these two young people fell in love and realized they had no real reason to be enemies. They broke that mold and that unbridled hatred cost everyone dearly.

Have you ever been bullied? Do you think of that bully as your enemy? If you think about someone who acts as a bully toward others, if you observe their behavior, you will very likely see someone who is very insecure and even hurt. There is an old expression – "Hurt people, hurt people." This means that when we are hurt by someone or something, we take that hurt out on others and cause them pain to match our own.

Try something if you have someone like that in your life and I promise you the results will very likely surprise you.

Try kindness.

Most bullies, enemies, will be disarmed by the kindness you show them. It will take some guts and perseverance and it may not work at once or even at all, but I'm willing to bet that it will change things. It might alter that person's unpleasant behavior toward you.

Frenemy:

This is a newer word that is a combination of the words, friend and enemy. It's what we call an oxymoron and refers to someone you're friendly with even though you have a fundamental dislike for or rivalry with. This can be someone you compete against in a sport or on the debate team or in subjects like math or science. This person could have the characteristics of both a friend and an enemy.

Some people act like your friend but exhibit signs that they don't always have your best interest at heart. Watch to see if your "frenemy" is jealous of your success. They can be oversensitive when challenged and can even seem to want to sabotage things for you when things are going too well for you. Frenemies often offer veiled insults about you or people in your life. They don't celebrate your wins and often dwell on your failings, making fun or challenging you and your abilities.

Frenemies love negative info and dig for information often pretending to care but seem to revel in your misery. They like to make "jokes" that serve to put people down, even in front of the person. Do you have a friend like that? They say things like "I was just kidding. Can't you take a joke?

While frenemies can be assets at times they may ultimately be detrimental to your progress and happiness.

Alliance/Ally:

You may have someone that is helpful to you but is not actually a friend nor are they an enemy. Your teachers are a good example of someone that might be a strong alliance – ally.

Allies are people with a common goal like teammates. You may not socialize with them, but you have each other's backs on the playing field.

Allies are happy when you succeed but they may not celebrate your successes with you. They have no reason to see you fail and good reasons to see you succeed.

The word Ally comes from the Latin word *alligare*, meaning "to bind to." In wartime, nations who are allies work together to beat a common enemy and protect one another.

In your lifetime, you will make some great allies. You will have people you work with who will help you grow, and it will benefit both of you when you do. If you get a job and find a mentor at the company that will help you navigate the parameters of the job, they benefit when you do well, especially if you are in their department or they are a supervisor of yours. When the team does well, everyone succeeds. You can be an ally for someone as well. The goal is for everyone to do well.

Friend:

Here's another secret I need to tell you. You will have very few actual friends in your life, and that's okay!

Social media has diluted the word friend. People who "friend" you on Facebook or Instagram are not necessarily actual friends. They're people who may know you a little or even a lot. The two Tanya's had a real friend. Tanya 1 disrespected that friendship and lost a true friend whereas Tanya 2 understood how valuable that friendship was.

You don't need a hundred or certainly a thousand friends. You need a couple and if you have even one friend that you can count on in any situation, one that will not judge you when you fail, will celebrate sincerely when you succeed and be there with you for the best and worst times of your life, consider yourself really lucky. If you have a couple of people in your life like that, you are truly blessed.

Cherish these people. Keep them close. Celebrate with them and be there for them in their darkest moments. These are the people that will hold you up your entire life.

Knowing and Setting Your Boundaries

Everyone has what we call boundaries. For some, those boundaries can be physical. We call that personal space and we don't like it when someone comes into the bubble we imagine that surrounds us. We have that crowded feeling when someone gets "in our face!" This means they are in our space.

But boundaries don't have to be physical. They can mean there are things we find acceptable and things we don't. Personal Boundaries are basic guidelines that help you determine how you want to be treated. By knowing them, you can educate the people in your life on how you would like them to behave around you.

Personal boundaries can mean any number of things like:

- Using profanity – you may not like to hear people curse around you or it may be okay with you
- Being disrespectful of others and older people
- Public displays of affection – holding hands may be okay with you but not kissing in public
- Rudeness
- What you are okay with posting on social media and what you are not
- Needing alone time and space
- When and where you find it acceptable to text and how much
- Whether it's okay to come over to your house without calling first
- Sharing passwords with a friend, boyfriend, or girlfriend or other relatives
- Reading private things like poems or a diary
- Sharing or borrowing clothes – siblings fight over this one all the time
- Borrowing your personal items, computer, car, collectibles, tools, art supplies, etc.

Borrowing things is a big issue when talking about personal boundaries. If someone "borrows" your homework on a regular basis, they may not be a really great friend and truthfully, neither are you.

What?!

Yup! You're doing what we call enabling that person. Later in life, that same friend will "borrow" all sorts of things if you don't set a boundary. They will "borrow" money, your car, your clothes, your favorite vintage albums, jewelry and just about anything you're foolish enough to "lend" them.

The problem is that most of those "borrowed" items will never be returned. Just like your homework, they will be taken. This is not borrowing and you're not helping them by letting them do that. You're making it easy for them to fail. They have no motivation to succeed and get their own things, study and do their own homework, not cheat on tests or in life.

This goes back to values. What are yours? If you value respect for yourself and others, you will set a boundary around you that rudeness will not be tolerated. If you value cleanliness, you will not allow people to trash your home and ruin your belongings. If you value privacy, you won't allow people to read your diary, have your passwords, post private pictures and share them on social media. You will know how to ask for quiet alone time to reflect and meditate and find your own center, your own peace.

First, you have to value yourself.

You have to know that you are **VALUABLE!**

Once you do, you can set reasonable, sensible boundaries and learn how to make others respect those boundaries without anger or dissention.

Navigating Your Inner Critic

Inside every one of us lives a critic, a little person in your head that talks to you all the time. It's not usually very nice or very kind. It tells you that you're too fat, you don't look good in that shirt, you're too stupid to pass that test, you're too ugly to get that girl to go out with you or that boy to notice you.

Oh! you thought only you had that voice?

WRONG! We all have that voice and it's really hard to SHUT IT UP!

But you can get control of it with some effort. You can do what we call self-soothe. If your voice tells you to panic because you're not prepared for that math test tomorrow, you can get it to quiet down in a couple of ways.

The first thing you can do is take 4 very deep breaths. Sit down and plant your feet solidly on the floor. Relax your shoulders. They are likely up around your ears. Get them to drop.

Let all the air out of your lungs and then breathe in while you slowly count to four. Hold the breath there for just a second, then let your breath our slowly while you count to seven.

Repeat that four times.

Exercising can help quiet the little voice. Take a run. Play a little basketball, take a bike ride, or do some yoga. If you concentrate on your body, you can quiet your mind.

If you're interested to learn how to meditate, that will be a huge help in learning how to shut out the negativity of the inner critic.

Some people recommend saying positive affirmations. You may love that or find it a little silly, but you can try it.

Repeating positive things can confuse the little critic.

- I'm smart and capable
- I'm attractive
- I'm kind to others
- My friends and family love me
- I'm a good and trustworthy friend
- I'm respectful
- I work hard at my studies
- I'm a good employee
- I matter

ZIZ ABDUR RA'OOF & LIL BARCASKI

Every time the little critic shoots his or her mouth off, tell it the opposite of the lies it's telling you. Yes, those are lies. The critic is a big old liar!

You can accomplish things, succeed at things, learn new skills, make friends, be a happy and productive person. But if you succumb to the critic in your head, you're going to make it a lot more difficult to do any of those things.

Building Your Circle of Influence

So, now you are starting to determine your values, you're setting your boundaries, and you're quieting the critic in your head. You know the difference between an enemy, a frenemy, an ally, and a true friend.

It's time to start to understand and build your circle of influence.

You will have allies, friends, and colleagues in your life, even in your days in school, even in high school, certainly in college and later in life. Your friends will always be part of your circle of influence. They will be trusted allies who will help you grow and succeed, and you will do the same for them. If you want to achieve something, they will be your first champions. You will share your talents with them, and they will do the same. When you need a support system, they will be the first people you ask for help and they you.

But there will be other people you meet that will be part of your circle of influence. Be kind and respectful to others because you may never know when someone can be the exact person you need later in life.

You will want to grow a strong circle of influence. The people you meet and connect with may not all become best friends or even friends at all but they can be people you can go to and trust when you need to learn something they know, meet someone in their circle of influence who can help you with your career, education, or life in general.

Here are a few key things to do to help open the door to finding and creating your circle of influence:

- Be proactive. Don't wait for people to come to you.
- Listen and pay attention to others.
- Be consistent.
- Be kind to everyone – it costs nothing, and that kindness may come back to you later on.
- Appreciate the people who help you and even the people who don't.
- Learn from EVERYONE because everyone has something to teach you.
- Take responsibility for your words, deeds, and actions.
- Learn to be sympathetic and empathetic and know the difference between the two.
- Ask questions and make note of the answers.
- Find what you are passionate about and pursue it vigorously.
- Always be learning and improving your skills
- Don't believe everything you hear – use good judgement.
- Be enthusiastic and excited about life.
- Follow up with people – check in with them and ask how you can help them.
- Take notes.
- Make lists of the people you connect with, how you met them, what they do, and how to reach them – phone numbers, email address, social media links, websites.
- Have the utmost integrity – be impeccable with your word (read *The Four Agreements*).
- Go the extra mile to help others and be your best self.

- Use your own influence to help others.

You're never too young to start what we talked about in this chapter. Start now to determine your values, find your friends, and allies. They will be your tribe. Start to build your circle of influence and don't let that inner critic talk you out of it, tell you you're not ready, or that you're wasting your time to do these things.

Chapter 8 Exercises:

Make a spreadsheet or list of as many people you are in contact with as possible. School mates, friends, teachers, mentors.

- What category are they in – Enemy, Friend, Frienemy, Alliance?
- Are any of them in more than one category?
- How do they influence your decisions?
- What value do they bring to your life?
- How does this knowledge help you to go forward toward success?

Talk to the people on the friends list or members of your family. Discuss your values and your personal boundaries with them. Ask them about theirs but don't judge them if theirs differ from yours.

There are lots of ways to think, live, and behave. Everyone has a right to choose their own values and beliefs.

Accelerate

THE BIG GIG ECONOMY

THE STORY OF TWO SAMS

Sam 1 took a class in robotics in 7th grade and fell in love with this subject. He started with simple electronics and learned about components and gears. He got to learn to program a small robot with his classmates. Over the years, he continued to learn about robots and electronics. He found a group of people who he met with and built all kinds of fun robotics projects all through college. But Sam decided he was going to use his math skills and become a high school math teacher.

The high school principal offered him a little extra pay to run a robotics club and he jumped at the chance. Lots of kids signed up for the club and they competed with other clubs and won prizes. Sam was proud to be able to use his skills and talents and teach his students how to make robots. A couple of his students went on to become experts in the field and he was proud to know he gave them a head start on something that was so important to the world. One of them even got a job at NASA.

Sam 2 took a class in robotics in 7th grade and fell in love with this subject. He started with simple electronics and learned about components and gears. He got to learn to program a small robot with his classmates. When he got to high school, his electronics teacher realized that he had a special gift when it came to this subject. That teacher went out of his way to get more and more information for Sam. Sam decided to build his own robot and he won a statewide contest on robotics. That helped him get accepted to MIT (Massachusetts Institute of Technology), one of the best schools in the country. He was offered a job at iRobot before he even graduated. iRobot was created by three MIT graduates and they were happy to employee Sam. He had his dream job and made his hobby his life work.

What is a "Gig?"

Musicians may have coined that phrase and by gig they are referring to jobs where they get paid to play. The expression – gig economy –

refers to the concept today, instead of just going to a 9 to 5 job, people are making their own jobs, their own "gigs."

Uber and Lyft drivers are in a sense part of the gig economy. People starting small businesses that they do as a full or even part time income generator are creating gigs for themselves.

People are piecing together work doing things they like, are good at, and can make them some money either as their only source of income or as part time, "side hustle." Something they do in their spare time, like evenings or weekends.

Why your older siblings, cousins, aunts and uncles (often called millennials) may be right.

Young people today are disgruntled and questioning the "way things have always been." Many years ago, if you got into a decent college, got good grades, and learned a particular subject/skill, you were likely to get a job in your field and start to make a decent salary.

That's not necessarily true today. There are no guarantees.

Moreover, we see more and more people becoming dissatisfied with the idea of going to a job every day and being a small part of a big corporation, or an expression your grandparents might have used, "a small fish in a big pond." But, there will always be bills to pay, and if someday you plan to have a family, there will be children to care for and feed.

Millennials are a different breed. These older brothers, sisters, cousins, young aunts and uncles of yours value experiences. They want to contribute to the work they're doing, have their ideas heard. They want to build things, create things, especially things that improve the lives of others and the health and wellness of the earth itself. They have good ideas, kind hearts, and sharp minds.

ZIZ ABDUR RA'OOF & LIL BARCASKI

So, even when they take a job in a company, they are likely to have a side hustle; something they do as a hobby that makes them extra money by utilizing a skill or talent they have that isn't needed at their corporate, pay the bills, job. Take note of this. You may want to follow in their footsteps.

Hobbies and Talents – How to Use Them to Your Advantage

What are your hobbies? What do you enjoy doing that's out of the scope of schoolwork?

For some people, playing an instrument is a hobby. They enjoy it but they don't want or expect to make music their career.

Here are some hobbies and talents that you might be able to use to your advantage: (note that most if not all of these could be full-time career options, but they don't have to be)

- Sewing
- Painting/art
- Wood working
- Coding websites
- Graphic arts
- Gardening
- Cooking
- Bird watching
- Stamp collecting
- Dancing
- Martial arts
- Writing/journaling
- Scrap booking

These are just a few things that you might do for fun or relaxation. You can probably name several more things and your hobby may or may not be on that list. So, how can you monetize your hobby?

If you play an instrument, you can work on bringing your skill to a level where you might join a band, play in the pit of an orchestra for local theater companies when they produce a musical, or even get good enough to be hired to do some studio work when your instrument is needed for a recording.

If you sing well enough, you could do all of the above or be a karaoke DJ a night or two a week, more if you love that work. Or if you just love music, you might learn to be a DJ for parties and events.

Cooking can be a full-time career or a side hustle. Some people love to bake and make baked goods to take to farmers markets and fairs, taking their hobby to the next level. That's considered a "cottage industry" and you don't need to have special licensing for that in most states.

Craft fairs are filled with people who make crafts and do art of all sorts. For some of those people, that's their livelihood. For others, it's a way to both enjoy their hobby and make some extra money.

How to Work Your Side Hustle

Let's assume that you have a career path you plan to pursue that you know will pay the bills and you will enjoy doing. One of a couple of things can be true.

You might have a job that takes up all of your working time and work energy and pays very well. This can be true of doctors, accountants, lawyers, people who get into management at work and have very little downtime for hobbies. They may take whatever free time they have for exercise, yoga, meditation, vacations, and just plain relaxing to take their mind off work. Some people are into gaming, some binge-watching shows on Netflix and Hulu.

But some people, even those with busy careers, enjoy some sort of hobby. They may never want or need to make money sewing, cooking, or gardening. If that's the kind of career you wind up with and are happy to have, we're happy if you're happy.

Many people start their careers on the low rung of that ladder we talk about. They work 40 to 50 hours a week and their salary doesn't afford them much room to do fun things. Also, they may not find their job mentally stimulating, maybe not even fun, but it pays the bills and puts food on the table.

That's where a side hustle can come in. If you've ever taken an Uber or Lyft ride, many of those people are working a side hustle. They have a 40 hour a week job elsewhere or they do something like real estate sales and can adjust their schedule or use their downtime to make some extra money driving people to the airport or delivering food. If you like to drive and like people, that could be a great side hustle.

Almost any hobby can bring in a little extra cash and a lot of extra fun. You just have to be creative, think out of the box, and learn to promote yourself. You may already be doing that.

Do you mow lawns or shovel snow for people in your neighborhood?

Do you make crafts and sell them at fairs and flea markets?

Do you collect stamps, coins, comic books or other collectable items that you can trade or sell?

Any of these things can be a side hustle now or later in life. Also, most hobbies can become your "GIG."

Making a Career by Doing the Thing You Love

You don't have to be Sam 2 to make your hobby or skill your career. You have to have tenacity and willingness to work hard. Nearly anything can be turned into a business, you just need to be clever.

Watch the show, *Shark Tank*. The one thing that the businesses that come on to pitch their ideas to the sharks, is the people who started the businesses saw a need for something that wasn't being addressed.

Sometimes it can be as simple as creating a better way to exercise. There are people making videos of exercise routines based on simple dance moves. If you love yoga, you might become a yoga instructor, but you can also create videos and set up a You Tube Channel that people can subscribe to where you offer simple yoga instruction.

If cooking or baking is your passion, you can do a number of things from cooking meals for people in their homes or for parties to starting a catering company. You can work in a bakery until you learn the business and start your own – maybe even start with a food truck.

Whatever you love to do, if you set your mind to be really good at it, it can become your life's work. It doesn't mean you have to work for someone else forever. You may have to work for someone until you learn the things you need to go out on your own.

But here's something to think about. If you have a talent, a skill, a hobby that you love and think someone will pay for the products you can make, or the talents you have, in the world we live in now, it doesn't take much to get started making money at it.

Remember we talked about using social media or making a website. Those are inexpensive ways to promote whatever business you create.

Check out this young lady who started this company at 11 years of age.

Mikaila Ulmer: A social entrepreneur, bee ambassador, educator and student.

Me and the Bees Lemonade www.meandthebees.com

Her story from her website:

When I was just four, my family encouraged me to make a product for a Children's business competition (the Acton Children's Business Fair) and Austin Lemonade Day. So, I put on my thinking cap. I thought about some ideas. While I was thinking, two big events happened.

- *I got stung by a bee. Twice.*
- *Then my Great Granny Helen, who lives in Cameron, South Carolina, sent my family a 1940's cookbook, which included her special recipe for Flaxseed Lemonade.*

I didn't enjoy the bee stings at all. They scared me. But then something strange happened. I became fascinated with bees. I learned all about what they do for me and our ecosystem. So, then I thought, what if I make something that helps honeybees and uses my Great Granny Helen's recipe?

Year-after-year, Mikaila, sells-out of her Me & the Bees Lemonade at youth entrepreneurial events while donating a percentage of the profits from the sale of her lemonade to local and international organizations fighting hard to save the honeybees. That is why she touts: Buy a Bottle...Save a Bee.

Now at age 14, when not at her lemonade stand telling all the digestive benefits of flaxseed, you can find Mikaila leading workshops on how to save the honeybees and participating in social entrepreneur-

ship panels. Mikaila launched her own Facebook page, where visitors can 'Like' interesting facts about bees, honey and Me & the Bees Lemonade.

Today, the award-winning Me & the Bees Lemonade is buzzing off the shelves of Whole Foods Market, the world's leader in natural and organic foods, and available at a growing number of restaurants, food trailers and natural food delivery companies.

All that from a couple of coincidences, a love for lemonade, and a desire to save the bees.

Inspired? Do the exercises!

Chapter 9 Exercises:

Do you have a hobby you wish you could earn a living at?

- Would it be a side hustle to your full-time job?

- Could it be a full-time job?

Research other people who are doing what you want to do or have similar interests. Use the power of Google.

Look up young entrepreneurs and see if any of them inspire you. Reach out to them through social media and ask if they might help you with your ideas.

Don't be afraid to ask questions. Mentors are everywhere. You just need to muster the courage to reach out to them.

10

HONING YOUR SUPERPOWER

EVERYONE HAS A SUPERPOWER... YES, YOU HAVE AT LEAST ONE yourself. The trick is to discover what those superpowers are. A superpower can be different from a talent. It's not necessarily something like your ability to play an instrument or being good at math. Think about superheroes and what powers they have; super strength, x-ray vision, being bullet proof, and being able to fly. Comic books are about far more than what you see on the surface. The superheroes powers are meant to reflect things about ourselves we all need to discover and hone as we grow up.

Super strength isn't just about being physically strong, it's about having fortitude, being able to hang tough in a crisis, being there for the people in your life who need you.

X-ray vision can mean being able to see through people, not to see their bones and organs, but to see when they are hurting, or lying, or afraid. What a great superpower that is to have and many people have it.

Being able to fly could mean being able to go far in life, to meet challenges, and be super successful. Maybe you're one of those people.

Discovering Your Superpower

What makes you special and even different from the people in your life? Are there ways in which you think you might be *super*?

- *Are you intuitive?*

Do you seem to know when someone is upset or in need of something. Can you sometimes guess what a person is thinking or perhaps know when someone you care about is afraid, lonely, sad, in need of your time? If so, your superpower might be – **Intuition and the super ability to care about others.**

- *Are you inquisitive?*

Do you love to learn new things and discover new paths? Do you ask questions, research, Google everything? If so, your superpower might be - **The ability to grow and expand your mind.**

- *Are you adventurous?*

Do you like to explore new places, new ideas, try new things? Are you the one in the family that will eat any kind of food, long to go to places you've never been, love to meet new people from all walks of life? If so, your superpower might be – **Exploration and a thirst for life.**

- *Are you strong?*

Not necessarily physically, but do you have strength of character?

Are you someone your friends and family can count on? Your super-power might be – **Fortitude and willpower.**

- *Are you kind?*

Do you like to help others, do random nice things for people, volunteer and be of use when others are in need? If so, your superpower might be – **The ability to empathize and change the world.**

Do you see what I mean by a superpower?

There are so many superpowers and they can include things like:

- Kindness, caring, and sensitivity
- Intelligence and loving to learn
- Having an artistic nature
- Loving to teach others
- Being a good friend and a good listener
- Being strong enough to take criticism and keep going and growing

Some superheroes seem to be born with certain gifts while others have to make the decision to challenge themselves and create their own strengths. Do you know the difference between the stories of two of the oldest superheroes in comic history, Superman and Batman?

Superman Versus Batman

Superman's home planet, Krypton, was about to explode. Superman, whose real name was Kal El, was put into a rocket by his parents and sent to Earth so he would be saved. On our planet, he had super-powers that he had to discover as he got older. He learned that he was super strong had super hearing, speed, x-ray vision, could fly, and most important he was bullet proof. The only thing that could hurt or possibly kill him, ironically, were pieces of his home planet that randomly fell to Earth.

Superman's powers were always there. He just needed to learn how to use and control them. And to protect himself and the people he loved, he sometimes had to pretend he didn't have those powers. He had to pretend he was a normal boy/man and so he lived part of his life as Clark Kent, taking the last name of the couple that found and raised him when he fell to earth.

Batman has a completely different story. Born into a wealthy family, young Bruce Wayne was coming home from the theater with his parents when they were brutally gunned down by a madman right in front of him. Fueled by his desire to avenge his parent's death, Bruce trained his body and his mind. He built his muscles while he built his amazing technology to help him fight crime. Thus, Batman was born. He too, had to hide part of his identity for security reasons.

Both of these men needed to protect their special powers and only bring them forth, change into their superhero costumes, when they were needed to fight crime and help humanity. Even we mere mortals have to learn to control our powers, not so much hide them, but protect them and use them for the good of others and ourselves.

Even superheroes have things that could hurt them the way Kryptonite can hurt Superman.

Learning What Your Kryptonite Is: and How to Deal with It

There are things that can hurt you, make you feel weak, sad, unhappy. You can't always avoid those things, but you can learn how to deal with them. You're going to have disappointments and heartaches, but you can learn to navigate those things and even use them to your advantage the way Superman learned how use his superpowers.

Most of us get bullied, teased, or have our feelings hurt. That can feel like Kryptonite is to Superman. As hard as it is, you will have to learn to ignore bullies and not believe the hurtful things people can sometimes say. Bullies are usually very unhappy people and their words have no meaning unless you give them meaning.

Sometimes, you will want something to happen, to pass a test, win a contest or game, have someone like you, but it doesn't happen. If not being able to fail or lose or not have things go your way is very difficult for you, like Batman, you will have to train hard. You will need to learn to fail well and lose gracefully.

Even if your superpower is being super smart, you're going to fail at some subject or at least struggle to learn some things. No one is good at everything. If something interests you but it doesn't come easily to you, think of Batman and train hard, educate yourself on that subject. Think of Superman and realize even he wasn't perfect. He had flaws too. He had his Kryptonite.

Find out what stops you from being your best self and work on knocking down the blocks that stand in your way. Don't be afraid to learn new things, try new things, hone your superpowers and your talents.

One of the great things about being you in the time that you are living is the fact that there are lots of ways to learn and lots of ways to educate yourself for free. There are so many free ways to learn if you have a computer or even a phone and the desire, the drive, and the ambition.

Free Education is Everywhere: Go Get It

We've talked about getting a mentor, growth mindset, and different ways to learn. Whether you want to explore, discover, find ways to grow, help others, be a better, stronger, smarter person you can find lots of free inspiration everywhere.

There is pretty much nothing you can't find a tutorial for on You Tube. There are videos on everything from how to change a tire, tie a tie, build a boat, bake a cake, or play almost any instrument. https://www.youtube.com/

There is a thing called Ted Talks and the people who are chosen to give a Ted Talk range from physicists to bird watchers, philanthropists to philosophers with subjects ranging from kindness to chemistry. And there are talks specifically made by and for younger people like yourself.

Here are links to some of those:

https://www.ted.com/playlists/86/talks_to_watch_with_kids

https://www.ted.com/playlists/129/ted_under_20

Some of these very inspirational young people may inspire you to consider how to discover and hone your own superpowers.

If you want to learn a subject of any kind, there are many online sources that offer free classes. Some will be very difficult, others not so much. Science, art, graphics, coding, web design, biology, physics, mathematics, all have teachers offering their talents to the world. Some of the classes can have a cost for people who want to get college credits, but most courses can be audited at low or no cost at all.

Here are a couple of online sources for free or cheap classes.

https://www.coursera.org/ - mostly free classes.

https://www.udemy.com/ - mostly cheap classes.

https://www.khanacademy.org/ All free classes for grade school through high school

Not free but very cool:

If you can have the budget for it, one of the best online course outlets is Master Class. Real experts in a variety of fields. This may be something for the whole family to enjoy and is likely better for high school and college aged students but worth exploring. There are over 80 classes, with an average of 20 lessons per class and each lesson is only about 10 minutes in length. Short, impactful, and to the point, these experts offer real-life advice, tips, and tricks of their trade.

On Master Class, the world's greatest experts teach lessons on:

- Writing
- Culinary Arts
- Business, Politics & Society
- Sports & Games
- Film & TV
- Music & Entertainment
- Design, Photography, & Fashion
- Lifestyle
- Science & Technology

https://www.masterclass.com/

You can also look for local classes being offered in your area too. Some of the community centers and even places of worship have classes you can take or talks you can attend.

If you're in high school and especially later when in college, you can seek internships. The job of an intern is typically unpaid but allows you to work with professionals in the field you think you might want to go into. Before you get to that place, do the work of discovering your superpowers, hone them and make sure they work with your talents. If you learn to marry your talents with your superpowers, you will be unstoppable.

Chapter 10 Exercises:

List at least one thing you think is your superpower. (more if you have a few)

What can you do because of that superpower(s)?

Identify 5 classes, courses, or videos that will help you sharpen your superpower or skills.

1. _____
2. _____
3. _____
4. _____
5. _____

Watch at least 3 Ted Talks that sound interesting to you.

11

WHAT'S YOUR VIBE?

When you think of energy — what comes to mind?

Ever go to a live musical event and the singer hits that note that's so powerful you get goosebumps? The performance is so awesome that you not only feel the energy — so does everyone else at the venue.

Everyone is vibing and it's contagious.

That's how I feel about Energy. Our energy arrives to a space before we do. How we appear in a space or even on social media impacts others or carries weight. Many times, friends have shared with me that I have a presence. It's especially noticeable when I'm not my typical jovial self or when I'm in deep thinking mode. I'm pointing this out because people can give off positive, neutral, or negative energy(vibes).

In a conversation with a friend, I asked her how she would define energy to her daughter. She defined it as "the vibe you get either positive or negative from people when you are in their presence and the vibe you give off too."

I decided to research the definition of the word energy, which led me to a synonymous word - (vibrations).

Vibrations. Informal. a general emotional feeling one has from another person or a place, situation

The latter part of the definition made me think about sports. I've been involved with games where I could feel the energy from my classmates who were packed in a gymnasium cheering us on to win. Once, while playing in a football game against Clemson we needed a touchdown to win the game but there was less than a minute and thirty seconds on the clock. Our team broke from the huddle and I ran out to my position as receiver to the wide side of the field. I was confident that I could easily run by the defender as I ran out to my position, only in my head I was thinking, *don't drop the ball, don't drop the ball.*

So, what do you think happened in front of 85,000 yelling fans and countless people watching on tv?

Yep, I dropped the ball because that's what I was thinking. I can still see the picture clearly in my mind today of that scenario.

Sidebar: (what should I have been saying to myself)?

Have you ever been in a situation (whether before a test, speech, drama/musical performance) that required you to perform at your best and you fell short because of not fully believing in yourself — You were not totally committed to it!

Sometimes we fall short despite our best efforts, however, the learning you gain from the experience is impactful and a teachable moment.

Famous individuals like Oprah, Sarah Blakely, Lizzo, Steve Jobs, and many others have used their personal and or professional disappointments to overcome adversity.

Understanding your own energy is critical to self-awareness. It'll give you the information needed as you go forth on your journey to becoming the best version of yourself. Understanding that energy is all around us is key to knowing how to operate in various situations. Sometimes, we bring about our own demise in low energy and sometimes we need a boost to our energy levels. It's key to understand that what we consume either in what we physically (eat or drink), (what we read or listen to), or who we surround ourselves with will have an impact on our being. We get to choose how we interact in the world and how we respond to the various stimuli in our environment.

How to Use Our Energy/Vibes

Here are the 5 steps how you can raise your vibration and use the Law of Vibration to manifest what you want in life:

- 1. Set a Clear Intention
- 2. Use Visualization
- 3. Use Your Emotions as if you've already accomplished it
- 4. Trust and Believe in the Process
- 5. Let Go and be Ready to Receive

Step One - Set a Clear Intention

Most people have no idea what they want, let alone setting a clear concise intention. A lot of people are too vague with their thoughts. At a moment, a student may want to audition for a high school play or musical, and at the next moment, they feel doubtful and prefer to continue stay in their comfort zone rather than stretch themselves into new and different experiences.

Step Two - Raise your Visualization

Visualization is one of the most powerful tools that can help you in this. When you visualize what you want, your mind cannot differentiate from what is real and what is being imagined. This is why when you visualize eating Chick-fil-A your mouth salivates, and you will have more saliva in your mouth. Your mind makes what you visualize real. Thus, practice visualizing the things that you want to be, do, and have in your life.

Step Three - Use Your Emotions as if you've already accomplished it

You need to raise your vibration to a higher level through your emotions too.

You cannot just dream about what you want and hope for things to happen. You need to feel it with your emotions. For example, do not just visualize what you want, you must associate your emotions and feelings into the process. Feel as if you are already successful. Feel as if you have achieved your goals and are living your dreams.

Your emotion is one of the most powerful tools that can elevate your vibration and help you manifest what you want in life. Without emotions, nothing moves.

Step Four - Trust and Believe in the Process

When you truly believe in something, you will never question it and you will do it. Yes, you will take action when you believe in something.

For example, remember the football example of me dropping the ball, I was confident in running past my defender, however, I had some doubt in catching the football. If you believe without a shadow of a doubt that you will own and have a successful business then you're going to succeed.

Do you think you will work on it? Yes, you will with a vigor and an intensity.

Most people do not believe that they can achieve their dreams and manifest what they want, this is why they are not taking action. All they do is to think about what they want, but deep within their hearts, they do not actually believe that it is possible for them. Never let this happen to you. Choose to trust the process and believe in it. More importantly, when you truly believe in it, you will act on it.

Step Five - Let Go and be Ready to Receive

Finally, you need to let go and be willing to receive. Do not be over obsessed with the things that you want. When you become so obsessed, you will feel stress the moment you don't receive the results you desire.

Most people are so obsessed with the result that this has created the opposite effect and caused the manifestation process to fail. Treat the manifestation process like planting a tree. All you need to do is to make sure that you water it daily. Make sure the plant receives enough sunlight and the soil is suitable for it to grow. After that, you just let go and believe that the plant will grow.

What do you think will happen if you over-water the plant? You will kill it. There is no need to rush for the result. You just need to believe in it and be willing to receive it when it arrives. Just like growing a plant, you do what you can, and believe in it. Somehow, the universe will work its magic and the plant will grow. The same applies to your dreams and the things that you want to realize in this world.

Willing vs Wanting

You are never

ever

ever

ever

ever

ever ......going to feel like doing the things you need to do, to get the things you want. In order to get those things you need, you must be willing to *push yourself*.

Typically, it's your (parents, grandparents, guardians) doing the pushing while you're under the age of 18 and living under their supervision. In other words, you may not be paying the majority of the bills to live. But this will change. Whether you want to our not, you will become an adult one day. Some people never fully embrace the idea of growing up. They want things in the way that children want things, but they may not be willing to do the hard work to get those things.

This is where the term "Failure to Launch" is applicable. Most children realize as they become teenagers and get older, that they would like to be their own person, not someone that relies on their parents or the adults in their lives forever. They realize that they want to make their own decisions, live in their own homes, drive their own cars, start their own kind of family. This is growth and it happens for most of us. Slowly, and while we are not fully aware of it, we begin to grow up. We begin to make "adult" decisions. As you get older, try to pay attention to those feelings. Try to recognize your growth spurts, not just the changes in your height or in your bodies, but in your attitude, in the way you take more and more responsibility for your own life and well- being.

Adulting

While you are in school, you have this adulting thing happening — someone telling you to clean your room, wash the dishes, do your homework, fill out your college applications, etc. Once you graduate high school and move onto the next stage of life, whether it's trade school, community college, and or living away from home at a college/university, or a job. The burden of pushing yourself shifts to your shoulders rather than the adult who was at times nagging you to do things. All of a sudden, you realize that feeling of being more independent, however, that feeling of not wanting to do things is still present. The popular author, talk show host and motivational speaker Mel Robbins said, "you will always need to push yourself and no one is coming." It's your job, your 18 and now it's your turn to parent yourself!

I'll end with my friend Bridget B's infamous quote "Everything costs something, are you willing to put forth the effort and energy to perform at the level needed to be the best version of yourself?"

Chapter 11 Exercises:

Meditation exercise:

Start with 3 minutes of meditation. Do that for one week.

Week two: Expand that to 5 minutes.

Week three: Meditate 10 mins per day.

Build the meditation muscles that will allow you to meditate regularly.

What things are you taking more responsibility for in your own life?

How do you see your life as an adult?

- Where would you live if you could live anywhere?

- What kind of home would you live in?

- What kind of car would you drive?

- What kind of food would you eat?

Accelerate

12

THE REAL F WORD

THE STORY OF TWO CASSANDRAS

Cassandra 1 was sad. She was dumped by her long-time significant other on her 27th birthday... at her own party, no less! She was humiliated and crushed. She crumbled and could not get out of bed for weeks. She ran out of sick days at her job and got fired. "Who cares," she thought. "I didn't like that job anyway." She stopped going to the gym and ate a LOT of ice cream. Her friends started to worry about her, but instead of letting them help her or seek their advice and assistance, she just told them to mind their own business. Soon, she had gained 20 pounds, could not pay her rent, or her car insurance or any of her bills.

Defeated and deflated, she had to move back home. Her mom and dad had turned her old bedroom into a craft room for mom, so she moved into their basement, took a part-time job at a flower shop, and wallowed in self-pity, often complaining that no one ever bought her any flowers. She got fired from that job after 6 months and over the years bounced from job to job, never making enough money to move out of her parent's house. Her friends stopped calling her. She ate a lot of fast food, didn't go out much, and spent most of her free time watching reality TV, browsing Facebook and Instagram (mainly to stalk her ex), and playing games online. She spent the rest of her life blaming that one break-up and the universe for her unhappiness and constant bad luck.

Cassandra 2 was sad. She was dumped by her long-time significant other on her 27th birthday... at her own party, no less! She was humiliated, hurt, and angry. She let herself cry it out, HARD, and lay in bed the rest of the weekend, eating ice cream and talking to her besties on the phone.

On Monday morning, she got up and dragged herself to work. As she sat at her desk, she suddenly realized that she really didn't like her job. That night, she asked her two best friends to meet her for dinner. She told them that she had always wanted to own her own business. They were thrilled to help and encouraged her to go for her dream. She listened to their advice and comments. She knew she could count on them and they talked through some of her ideas and helped her form a plan to make some real changes in her life. She joined a gym and started eating more healthy foods now that she was cooking only for herself. She took a class on how to start a small business and read every book she could find on how to become a successful entrepreneur. She attended seminars and workshops and on her 28th birthday, one year to the day of her ugly break-up, she quit her job because she had already started her new business as a side hustle and was making more money at that than she was at her 9 to 5 day gig. As she packed her desk up, she smiled and thanked the universe for what turned out to be the best thing that ever happened to her.

The real F word is *Failure!*

It's a word some of us dread hearing. Yet, it can indicate Failure and Success. They are on the same road, yet one is just a bit further down the road.

Here's a great example - learning to ride a bike. Do you remember taking off the training wheels and having your mom, dad, or sibling run beside you, holding the seat as you pedaled? When they let go, you most likely veered off into the grass or pavement.

But do you remember what happened next?

You got back up on the bike and did it again, and...

again and...

again and...

again...

and again until you could pedal without any help or support. You continued until you got comfortable. You kept at it without hesitation until you got really good at it. You wanted to master it, so you kept failing until you gained success. Your vision was clear. You could see yourself riding your bike solo and feeling jubilation, freedom.

Imagine if we approach life by embracing failure as a companion to success. Failure and Success are neighbors on the same side of the street of life.

I love this quote by Tom Bilyeu:

"Failure is a gut check to find out if you believe enough to push forward even when the world seems to be telling you not to."

I love Tom Bilyeu's quote because it causes you to pause, think and question - What's at the core of you?

Below are examples of things we say to ourselves (our inner dialogue) or that internal voice that pops up and says:

"Oh, I should just quit, it's too hard."

"Oh, I am not good enough."

"Oh, I am not worthy."

"Oh _____."

I remember having that internal dialogue in college when I was recovering from my achilles injury. It was my first time missing a game let alone a season due to a major injury. The initial news hit me hard at halftime when the doctor said, "Yep, you have ruptured your achilles tendon and will miss the rest of the season."

We were 3-0 at that point and I was the leading receiver on the team. Kaboom - season over - lots of thoughts went through my head during that time as I showered and shed a few tears. My life took an abrupt change, I went from being an able bodied athlete to someone needing support to simply get out of the shower and down the steps. (I am not able to name everyone, however, there are a few friends who were there for me that stood out -Duane Dunham, Mike Echols, Mickey Stoffel, Chris Bobo, Monique McAlpine, Mary Rejevich and Ken Schneider.)

Let's just say, I needed to get back up and ride the proverbial bike again, only I needed to start with training wheels and graduate to going without them. This was a gut check for me, it required me to rely on people in a way I had never done before in my life. I am grateful to the many people who supported me in many ways, from those who carried my lunch tray to the dining table to those who walked with me to class and held the door open. You learn a lot about yourself when you are tested in a different way in life.

The road to recovery for me was long, however, it reinforced the idea that success and failure are on the same side of the road. Success can be a bit further down the road and requires a lot of work (mental, physical, emotional and spiritual work). We live in a society where the highlights are emphasized; just think ESPN, a sports network that focuses on highlights. We don't hear much about what it took for people to become successful or make an impact.

There are quite a few famous people who have made an impact on society in various ways. All of them had bumpy roads on their way to their success.

Did you know Oprah Winfrey (she had two names back then) was fired from her TV anchor job in Baltimore before she became Oprah.

Thank goodness, Steve Jobs was fired from Apple because he went onto Pixar and NeXT and continued on with his vision to make his former company into a household name. Jobs return to Apple lifted them out of despair, and turned the company around into what that are today.

Eight time Grammy nominated "Lizzo" (Melissa Jefferson) lived out her car for months and almost quit music. In 2017, Lizzo released "Truth Hurts," the first single from her 2019 album, "Cuz I

Love You," but was so discouraged by the lack of response that she contemplated quitting music again. A month after releasing the album in May, it peaked to the Number one spot on the Billboard Chart.

"The song that made me want to quit, is the song that everyone's falling in love with me for," Lizzo told People Magazine, "which is such a testament to journeys: Your darkest day turns into your brightest triumph."

Sarah Blakely, Founder and CEO of Spanx, was named In 2012, by Forbes as the youngest self-made woman billionaire in the world. Yet, Blakey's best career advice came from her dad, who would ask in her high school years, "What did you fail at this week?"

He didn't want to know how many A's she had gotten. He wasn't interested in how many girl scout cookies she'd sold, how many goals she'd scored on her soccer team, or whether she'd gotten a perfect score on her math test. No, he wanted to know what she had failed at.

And when she told him, do you know what his reaction was?

He high-fived her.

There are many many people who we *could* list as famous failures – Dr. Seuss, JK Rowling, Tyler Perry, Kobe Bryant, Lebron James, Tom Brady, Gail Becker, and many others. I want to spotlight another who epitomizes what it means to dream and aspire despite circumstances.

- Dr. Seuss's first book was rejected by 27 different publishers.
- Tom Brady lost 3 Super Bowls
- JK Rowling was depressed, on government assistance, and her book was rejected twelve times before going on to

become the first person to earn a billion dollars writing children's books.

- Kobe Bryant missed 13, 766 shots during his career
- Lebron James lost 5 NBA Finals

I want to spotlight another who epitomizes what it means to dream and aspire despite circumstances.

A Story of Perserverance

In 2014, Maryam Mirzakhani, former Stanford mathematician and Fields Medal winner, became the first and only female winner of the Fields Medal since its inception in 1936. The Fields Medal is the most prestigious award in mathematics, and is often equated in stature with the Nobel Prize. Maryam was born in Iran and grew up at a time of the Iran-Iraq war. In an interview, Maryam told Quanta Magazine in 2014, that she did not grow up wanting to become a mathematician. As a child, she loved to read and make up stories and thought she might be a writer.

One of her middle school teachers told her that she was not at all talented in math and should never consider a career where math was involved. Despite this discouragment, she still had an interest and passion for math. As Maryam continued her education, another teacher took the time to see her hidden talents and championed and supported her passion for math. In high school, with the support of her principal, she and her close friend Roya Beheshti became the first female members of their Iranian Mathematical Olympiad high school team.

Maryam lost her battle with breast cancer a few years ago at the age of 40. The loss feels personal to many women in mathematics. "My mailbox is full of messages from other women," said Ingrid

Daubechies, a math professor at Duke University. "Women mathe-maticians all over the world are e-mailing each other, trying to comfort each other. It is heartbreaking that we had to lose a gifted mathematician and wonderful role model so soon."

Maryam continued on with that belief that Tom Bilyeu referenced in that quote I mentioned. She overcame her childhood experience of war, cultural issues, and a language barrier to become a great math-ematician that inspired other women to pursue math and science.

Embrace Failure and play the long game like these individuals.

Just imagine being told that you "lack imagination and have no good ideas." That's exactly what an editor told Walt Disney. If he had listened and quit, we would have no amusement park named Disney World or the numerous productions like Aladdin, The Lion King or Mulan from Disney productions.

Walt Disney stated…

"I think it's important to have a good, hard, failure when you're young because it makes you kind of aware of what can happen to you. Because of it, I've never had any fear in my whole life when we've been near collapse and all of that. I've never been afraid."

Embrace the F word like Walt Disney and the many individuals listed above. Playing the long game means thinking about more than today. It means getting back on the bike when you fall off, because you can see yourself, wind in your face, tires spinning, feeling the freedom of movement, only this time learn faster as you fail.

Get back onto your proverbial bike and ride toward your success. In other words... FAIL Faster toward YOUR Success.

Rebounding from Failure

"Success is knowing that you could be a millionaire and lose everything one day but be able to get it all back the next."

Don't let your emotions get involved when you fail at something. Wallowing in your mistakes is a time suck. It doesn't change or fix things and it doesn't help you fail *toward* your success.

Don't make excuses either.

If I had more time

If I had more money

If he/she had helped me more

If Mom had just done it with/for me

If... If... If...

Own your mistakes. Own your decisions, good or bad. Own your failures. They're yours and they are actually your best friends because they can help you eliminate things. They can shape who you are actually going to be. They can squarely place you on the right road.

Changing Your Mind is A-okay

You can do that, yup! You can go all through high school thinking you want to be a doctor and then fall in love with writing, or music, or law. Did you know that the average person changes careers seven times in their lifetime? Not just jobs, CAREERS!

If you find the thing you love, the thing that fuels and excites you, and you become whatever you become, enter whatever field, find the perfect career, and stick to it… great!

But if you change your mind every three months all through high school and get to college and still have a change of heart, that's A-OK!

Sometimes, out of nowhere, something finds us. Something strikes a chord in our soul and says, "Pick Me!"

I have met people who thought all they wanted was to be an athlete, an engineer, a teacher and then by some stroke of fate, they see a film, hear a lecture, read a book, meet someone who introduces them to something they never knew of or took interest in before and they are struck. They are smitten.

Change is good. Don't be afraid to walk towards the things that grab you and get hold of you.

The people who embrace change, change the world!

What is Grit?

Grit is a combination of three things, and you can learn all three.

- Perseverance
- Resilience and
- Self-soothing

Check out this excellent Ted Talk by Angela Duckworth on Grit - https://www.ted.com/talks/angela_lee_duckworth_grit_the_power_of _passion_and_perseverance?language=en

Perseverance simply means to persist. Keep going. There's an old expression, "When you're going through hell, keep going!" I promise you, there are going to be times when you are going to go through hell. Like all things you go through, you will get to the other side.

Have you ever swum in the ocean? If you have or ever get the chance to, there will be waves. Some will be small and easily gotten over, but some will be big and scary, and you will see them coming and start to panic.

But don't!

When a wave is too big to stand and brace though or jump over, put your head down and go through it. In a minute, it will wash over you and you will come out the other side and into the light.

Resilience means growing a thicker skin, learning to accept disappointments, lose, fail, get hurt and still keep going. It takes time and some people admittedly have more resilience than others. But you can learn it like riding a bike. You can learn to fall and still brush yourself off and try again.

Self-soothing is harder. Learning to calm yourself down, take deep breaths and know that nothing stays the same is a practiced art. Do you ever feel so sad that you want to cry? Did you know that when you are crushed, devastated by something that if you let yourself cry and I mean cry hard for just 90 seconds, you will feel better?

Breathe. Take 4 deep long breaths and remember that the world is constantly rotating. When you feel like a failure, like you're worthless, or lost… those are just feelings. Feelings can change on a dime.

School is hard. High school can be tough to navigate. College can be challenging.

And life… well, life is kind of a game and you can win that game.

You're IN THE GAME!

You can and will ACCELERATE!

FINAL WORDS!

You are the author of your own story.

You get to create it.

Set out daily to becoming the best version of YOU.

David Coleman, CEO of College Board suggests these three things that can support you toward having a transformative experience beyond high school and college.

- 1. Find great teachers and mentors (even one will do)
- 2. Engage in activities outside the classroom that provide experience and insight into your being.
- 3. Learn to love ideas, even when it hurts.

School isn't just about grades, it's about the habits you create. It's what you do to invest in yourself. It's about owning up to your choices and becoming the kind of person you want to be. It's about the skills, character, and network you build as you go forth in Life. It's about the relationships you forge.

Dr. Meg Jay calls it "Identity Capital" in her book titled, "Why your twenties Matter." Dr. Jay describes it as "the currency we use to metaphorically purchase jobs and relationships." Erik Erikson defines "Identity Capital" as the collection of skills, relationships, and professional resources we build up over our lives.

Accelerate your way to your Identity Capital (IC)! Drop me a line via IG on ways you are building up your IC.

We hope this book has opened up some possibilities for you. We want you to succeed, to be everything you want to be. We're behind you 100% and so are a lot of people.

As you go through high school and college and into your life you're going to have wins and losses. You're going to have good days and bad and your feelings may change day to day but remember feelings are just that... feelings.

Share them!

Share your happiness. Share your sorrow. When you're feeling good, enjoy it and let other's know. Find your tribe, the people that will be with you through good and bad, that you can turn to in every situation.

If you're having bad feelings, dark thoughts, or feelings of worth-lessness, reach out to someone and share those feelings too. There are people, sometimes even people you wouldn't expect, who will help you get through those feelings to the other side. Think of those bad feelings like a wave, one that seems too big and will crush you. If you learn to swim through those waves, you will also learn that when you get through them, you will come out into the sunshine on the other side.

Final exercises:

Write your own Story - you are the narrator, the star...

Be a star in your own Production.

What movie will you write if you think of your life as a script?

Who is the protagonist (hero), antagonist (bad guy), and who will be in the supporting cast?

What does success mean to you?

What does it feel like?

Final Words!

RESOURCES

The Four Agreements by don Miguel Ruiz

Plutchik's Wheel of Emotions -
https://www.6seconds.org/2020/08/11/plutchik-wheel-emotions/

U.S.A. Memory Championship -
www.usamemorychampionship.com

Memory and Brain Power Course -
www.maximummemorymastery.com

Grass Roots Leaders: The Brainsmart Revolution in Business
by Tony Buzan; Tony Dottino; Richard Israel

National Suicide Prevention Lifeline
Hours: Available 24 hours. Languages: English, Spanish.
1-800-273-8255

Teens in Crisis Help Hotline - https://teencentral.com/help/

Teens Helping Teens - Connect, talk, get help! -
https://teenlineonline.org/

Active Minds: www.activeminds.org

Active Minds is the nation's leading nonprofit organization promoting mental health awareness and education for young adults. Through education, research, advocacy, and a robust presence on high school and college campuses as well as workplaces, they are changing the culture around mental health.

Starting with one chapter in one dorm room, Active Minds now has a presence in 800 communities across all 50 states and directly reaches more than 1 million young people each year.

Through signature programs including the National Chapter Network, the nationally acclaimed Send Silence Packing exhibit, and compelling Active Minds Speakers, Active Minds is creating communities of support and saving lives.

- Suicide is the second leading cause of death for young people ages 10-24. *(National Institutes of Mental Health, Statistics, Suicide, 2017)*
- 67% of young adults tell a friend they are struggling before telling anyone else. *(Framework for Campus Mental Health Promotion and Suicide Prevention, Presented as part of an invited symposium at the SAMHSA Campus Suicide Prevention Grantee Technical Assistance Meeting, Gaithersburg, MD, January 2007)*
- 280 people decide not to go through with a suicide attempt for every person who dies by suicide. *(National Action Alliance for Suicide Prevention and the National Suicide Prevention Lifeline, Be The On T0, 2020)*
- 50% of cases of mental health issues begin by age 14; 75%

begin by age 24. *(National Institutes of Health (NIH), Age of onset of mental disorders: A review of recent literature, April 2008)*

* One in five adults has a diagnosable mental illness. *(National Institutes of Mental Health, Statistics, Mental Illness, 2017)*

Favorite Quotes

"One important key to success is self-confidence. An important key to self-confidence is preparation."

– Arthur Ashe, Professional Tennis Player

"Every great dream begins with a dreamer. Always remember, you have within you the strength, the patience, and the passion to reach for the stars to change the world."

– Harriet Tubman

"Don't let what you cannot do interfere with what you can do."

– John Wooden

"Let the child be the scriptwriter, the director and the actor in his own play."

- Magda Gerber

"Strive for progress, not perfection."

– Unknown

"Elegance isn't solely defined by what you wear. It's how you carry yourself, how you speak, what you read."

Carolina Herrera, Designer

"Most of us aren't performing at the level of our potential, we are performing at the level of our preparation."

- Steven Furtick

"I don't think being beautiful takes away from your credibility."

- Soledad O' Brien, Journalist

"Every time you state what you want or believe, you're the

first to hear it. It's a message to both you and others about what you think is possible. Don't put a ceiling on yourself."

– Oprah, CEO, OWN

"Nothing in life is to be feared. It is only to be understood. Now is the time to understand more, so that we may fear less."

- Marie Curie, Physicist

"I don't mind that you think slowly but I do mind that you are publishing faster than you think."

- Wolfgang Pauli, Scientist

"I am lucky that whatever fear I have inside me, my desire to win is always stronger."

– Serena Williams, Professional Tennis Player

"Every next level of your life will demand a different you."

— Leonardo Dicaprio, Actor

"No person is your friend who demands your silence or denies your right to grow."

– Alice Walker

―――――――――

"If you're going through hell, keep going." - Winston Churchill.

ACKNOWLEDGMENTS

Ziz's:

Writing a book is harder than writing a term paper because it never seems to end, and you are not writing for a grade. The writing process has been more rewarding than I could have ever imagined. None of this would have been possible without my "87" Tribe.

I am not able to name everyone and risk the chance of forgetting those who have supported me during this journey. Even though, you may not have been named, just know that over the last few years most everyone I have encountered in a school building, volleyball court, football field or dance performance have contributed to this book in some manner.

Thank you to Michele Pittel, Courtney & Michael Pachuta, Chris & Steve Powers, Cara Cragun, Pam Roy, Tina Mayes, Geri Cvetic, Tina Mayes, Lori Chessen Hinds, Kevin Clark, Melissa Bajadek, Andrea Sporre, Phyllis Fagel, Quay Holland, Nuria Williams, Sarah Daniels, Gina & Jon Gordon, Julia Bruck, Carolyn Havens, Molly Geil, Danielle Siebert, Kim Kolarik, Marjie Fudali, Shawn Lightfoot,

Darren Burns, Abby Ward, Taricio Simms, Arbrey Butler, Lara Mish, Laura Gilchrist, Lee Anderson, Carol Ann McCurdy, Carrie Bittman, Bob Choat, Suzy Fauria, Ann Rogers, Jennifer Girardi McCloskey, and Tom Terranova.

A very special thanks to my immediate "87" family. Thank you Mom, Dad, Fatimah, and Bridget. And to my special gifts, my children: Jamil, Saarah and Jordan.

Peace be with you, Ziz

> *What you think,*
> *You Become.*
> *What you feel,*
> *You Attract.*
> *What you imagine,*
> *You Create.*
> *- Buddha*

Lil's:

- Cyndi Long for her partnership and ever constant friendship and our awesome book graphics and powerful cover design.
- Katelyn Stewart who jumped in both feet to make this book a reality.
- All our beta readers who helped us make important changes.
- Tony and Michael Dottino for their many valuable contributions.
- My brother Steve – always my inspiration. See you on the other side.
- Both of my parents who were two of the finest educators that ever lived and to teachers everywhere. You are heroes and heroines. Keep doing the hard work.

ABOUT THE AUTHORS

Ziz Abdur Ra'oof - NFL Alum, Performance Coach, Speaker, Podcaster &
Education Consultant

Ziz was born and raised in Maryland and has been coaching students
from middle school to college aged students for more than a decade.
Ziz has always had big dreams as far back as middle school. Early in

life, with the support and help of his tribe, he recognized his gifts and the opportunities placed in front of him.

One of those proud opportunities came in high school when his hard work paid off and he earned a collegiate scholarship to represent the state of Maryland in football. This led to him reaching a childhood dream of becoming an NFL player, entrepreneur, father of three, and now a first-time author. During that journey, he faced many hurdles and barriers along the way, but always stayed true to himself.

These days you'll find Ziz speaking, mentoring, and coaching students, coaching wellness and teaching Yoga Sculpt in the community.

*Lil Barcaski - Writer/Blogger/Coach, Vice President of
LongBar Creative Solutions - LongBarCreatives.com and
Head Word Wrangler at GhostwritersNetwork.com*

Lil Barcaski has been a self-starting entrepreneur for her entire 30 plus year career. She has a diverse background, having owned, and operated successful restaurants and catering companies, and working in food and beverage management in major hotels as well as being a highly trained performer. Lil has also trained speakers using acting techniques and skills to help speakers hone their stage presentations. For the last 15 years, Lil has been the CEO and project manager of a web technology company and a much sought-after ghostwriter. A many time published author of top selling fiction and non-fiction, Lil has written and ghostwritten dozens of books in the business, memoir, young adult, and adult fiction genres. She is a professional blogger and web content writer and heads up a staff of writers, ghost-writers, editors, and publishing experts.

FOOTNOTES

Chapter 2:

Questions:

Name 5 things and/or people that are the biggest influencers in your life. This can be a person like a teacher or relative, it could be a type of music you listen to, or the kinds of movies you watch.

What are the first 5 things that come to you when you hear the word stress?

What is the one thing you want most from your parents?- **Grass Roots Leaders:** The Brainsmart Revolution in Business by Tony Buzan; Tony Dottino; Richard Israel

Chapter 7:

In doing research, I came across some principles from the cofounder (Adam Robinson) of The Princeton Review (p.13). Adam makes a few points that I wholeheartedly agree with based on my experiences working with students in schools. In his book "What Smart Students Know," Robinson states that the real secret between a smart student and others is **attitude**. Being a smart student means taking charge and teaching yourself. Becoming a smart student means taking responsibility for your education. No school can teach you the way you learn best, so how much you learn and how well you do is up to you.

(What Smart Students Know, p. 12) Smart students have different skills, goals, habits, priorities and strategies because they see school, the learning process, and even themselves differently. Being a smart student means taking charge and teaching yourself. Becoming a smart student means taking responsibility for your education. No school can teach you the way you learn best, so how much you learn and how well you do is up to you.

Chapter 11:

This was Kept Secret by Monks | It Takes Only 4 Days Dandapani May 9, 2019 YouTube - How do you get better at concentration? Simply — You start by focusing on one thing a time and the best way to get better at concentration is by integrating the practice into your life!

The Best Advice About Life You've Ever Heard | Dandapani Motivational Speech August 29, 2018 YouTube

This was Kept Secret by Monks | It Takes Only 4 Days Dandapani May 9, 2019 YouTube

The Best Advice About Life You've Ever Heard | Dandapani Motivational Speech August 29, 2018 YouTube

Chapter12:

Lizzo

https://www.cnbc.com/2020/01/24/lizzo-dropped-out-of-college-and-lived-in-her-car-before-singing-fame.html

Sarah Blakely

https://www.inc.com/melanie-curtin/billionaire-ceo-sara-blakely-says-these-7-words-are-best-career-advice-she-ever-got.html

Gail Becker

https://www.createcultivate.com/blog/career-advice-gail-becker-caulipower

Maryam Mirzakhani

https://info.umkc.edu/unews/celebrating-women-in-stem-dr-maryam-mirzakhani/

https://news.stanford.edu/2017/07/15/maryam-mirzakhani-stanford-mathematician-and-fields-medal-winner-dies/

https://www.scientificamerican.com/article/mathematics-world-mourns-maryam-mirzakhani-only-woman-to-win-fields-medal/

http://mathshistory.st-andrews.ac.uk/Biographies/Mirzakhani.html

Final Words:

David Coleman, CEO Collage Board
https://www.theatlantic.com/ideas/archive/2019/05/david-coleman-stop-college-admissions-madness/589918/

The statistic that should worry us most is this one: According to a 2014 study by Gallup and Purdue University, only 3 percent of students have the kind of transformative experience in college that fosters personal success and happiness. The 3 percent of students whose lives changed for the better—who, according to Gallup, had the types of experiences that "strongly relate to great jobs and great lives afterward"—had three features in common: a great teacher and mentor, intensive engagement in activities outside class, and in-depth study and application of ideas.

These three shared features are all about intensity—not just participation in college life, but active engagement. They require students to move beyond merely doing something and toward becoming devoted to something. They require a depth of commitment that will serve students well throughout their lives.

Mel Robbins - Parent yourself

https://youtu.be/JoQEY2sIMTg

CPSIA information can be obtained
at www.ICGtesting.com
Printed in the USA
LVHW022317291020
670158LV00006B/118

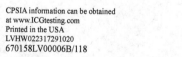

9 781733 692946